Praise for *Rising Tides*

"Like Google Maps, Neil Cole guides us past traffic jams of increased secularism and hostility to the gospel. He identifies a 'bridge to nowhere,' then paves the road to effectiveness for a church that has lost its way. His directions are simple, biblical, and will guide you to God's destination for you and your church. Neil has accomplished the near impossible—he's combined a strong prophetic warning with an extremely uplifting outcome."

RALPH MOORE
Author of *Making Disciples* and *How to Multiply Your Church*

"*Rising Tides* is Neil Cole's best book yet (and they are all good!). I simply couldn't put it down. Absolutely riveting, because he's absolutely right! He has pointed out the root issue facing the church in the West. The way we are prosecuting church is not just increasingly irrelevant for those who are not susceptible to being congregationalized; we simply aren't preparing people for the world they confront every day *now*, much less the *future*. If we don't make a culture shift from church-as-institution to church-as-movement, we will be sunk by the forces of the rising tide of massive discontinuity. 'It's not your fault,' I recently told a group of church leaders, 'for the growing societal allergic reaction to institutional religion. But it is our failure if we do not grow followers-of-Jesus who live as viral kingdom agents, who view and live life as a mission trip.' This book will help you do just that! Come on, get wet!"

REGGIE MCNEAL
Author of *Kingdom Come* and *Kingdom Collaborators*

"As Bob Dylan said, 'You don't need a weatherman to know which way the wind blows.' We all know the axis of global culture is tilting dramatically. We can feel it. But we do need a weatherman to show us not only how to survive these seismic shifts in our society, but to thrive and fulfill God's calling on our lives. Neil Cole's storm warning is just that—a winsome, biblical, and inspiring plan for a future-proofed faith."

MICHAEL FROST
Morling College, Sydney, and author of *Exiles* and *Incarnate*

"In his books as well as his ministry, Neil Cole has proven himself to be an exceptional apostolic practitioner, an original thinker, and a biblical scholar, as well as an artist and a novelist to boot. Now he reveals himself as something of a prophetic futurist, recalling the Church to its ancient destiny to be a transformative force in the 21st century. A worthy read."

ALAN HIRSCH
Author of *The Forgotten Ways* and *5Q*, and founder of Forge and 100Movements

"Neil Cole expertly describes converging trends and casts a prescient vision for the future. The result is a startling, inspiring, challenging, and hopeful call to the Church to embrace these trends as a catalyst to rediscover her core identity."

JESSIE CRUICKSHANK
Co-author of *Activating 5Q*, and 100Movements lead driver

"Neil does it again! Neil takes us on a tumultuous ride in his book, *Rising Tides*, as he addresses the dramatic waves we all are facing. He prophetically lays out how we can wisely navigate the current culture with principles within our reach and also create exponential movements with simplicity."

DAVE GIBBONS
Author of *Small Cloud Rising*, *Xealots*, and *The Monkey and the Fish*

"A frighteningly accurate wake-up call to the times in which we are living. Just glance through the table of contents and you'll see a world you recognize, whether you want to or not. Yet Neil's vision is not one without hope. He incorporates ideas for positive, concrete actions we can take. It's not fatalism; it's a call to the battle. Chapter nine and ten alone are well worth the price of the book—they cover the essential elements of a multiplication movement and provide many clear strategies that could be immediately implemented. Neil provides a hopeful way forward that will work in today's world."

DR. ROBERT E. LOGAN
Author of *The Missional Journey* and *The Discipleship Difference*

"Neil Cole looks past the present and into the future to alert us to changes that affect the Church and the way we do ministry. Neil brilliantly plays the part of a futurist in *Rising Tides* as he helps us navigate the dicey waters of change that are ahead."

DAVE FERGUSON
Pastor of Community Christian Church, author of *Hero Maker*
and *Exponential*

"There are very few people qualified to write a book like this, and Neil Cole is one of them. This book educates, challenges, and ultimately gives us a very real hope for the future. Neil provides us with both the warning and the clear solution, all in one hard-hitting volume."

KEITH GILES
Author of *Jesus Untangled*

"If you want to make disciples who make disciples who make disciples, read *Rising Tides* by Neil Cole. The principles of life change and transformation are simple to follow, easily reproducible, and can even be practiced by people who are not Christians."

JEREMY MYERS
Author of *Nothing But The Blood of Jesus*

RISING
TIDES

Also by Neil Cole

Cultivating a Life for God

TruthQuest

Organic Church

Organic Leadership

Ordinary Hero

Church 3.0

Journeys to Significance

Church Transfusion (with Phil Helfer)

Primal Fire

One Thing

RISING
TIDES

Finding a Future-Proof Faith in
an Age of Exponential Change

NEIL COLE

Cover and interior design by David Provolo

Edited by Val Gresham

ISBN: 978-0-9906604-8-4 (soft cover)
ISBN: 978-0-9906604-9-1 (e-book)

For Dezi Baker

My fellow change instigator, holy trespasser,
and "time-agent from the future."
Together we have journeyed from the gates of heaven
to the gates of hell...and back.
"Because you dare..."

CONTENTS

Time And Tide Wait for No One

I'd rather be an optimist and a fool than a pessimist and right.
—Albert Einstein

I never think of the future—it comes soon enough.
—Albert Einstein

ONE INTERESTING PIECE OF TRIVIA from my time working as a lifeguard at Venice Beach is this: I may be the only lifeguard to ever make an ocean water rescue *behind* his tower.

Extremely high tides, often called "super tides," can be incredibly dangerous and can wreak disaster along the coast, especially because they are often joined by high surf and wind. During the winter of 1983, strong storm surf combined with super tides washed away the entrance to the pier where my tower was. The tower remained unharmed atop the pier, but normal access to it was gone. The following summer, we had to park next to the pier and climb onto our truck's roof to be able to get up to the pier and then the tower.

The Pacific, however, was not finished with her fury. Later in the summer we received another round of super tides mixed with high surf. At the height of this occurrence, a river of water was channeled around the back of the tower and the missing pier entrance. One morning as I was waiting to cross this river to report for work at my tower, I heard my associate call out my name over the roar of water. I looked up, and he pointed to a small boy who had fallen into the river and was about to pass in front of me. I hadn't checked in yet, so I didn't have my rescue can (a flotation device with a strap to carry victims to shore). My partner threw a rescue can high into the air. It plopped in the water as I dove in, and I was able to grab it and seize the boy in one motion. The strong current was rushing the two of us toward the ocean, but a chain-link fence, erected to keep people from climbing onto the broken-down pier, had become mangled and now formed a dangerous, underwater steel net that was about to snare both of us. Using all my strength, I pulled myself and the boy out of the tidal river, just before we were caught in the sharp wire clutches of that barrier. We emerged unharmed alongside the pier.

Extreme tides are a force that nothing can stop. As the old saying states, "Time and tide wait for no one." It appears we are racing against both time and some rising super tides of exponential growth in our world today.

Perilous times

A tidal wave, or tsunami, can destroy an entire region and devastate a nation. There are some extreme tides rising in our world today that we are powerless to stop. This book addresses four exponential trends that are tidal waves lifting us ever higher and setting us up for a crushing break. The universal Church currently floats atop these rising tides, unaware of how serious the predicament has become. This is a wake-up call to God's people who must shift to meet the demands of these perilous times and understand the precious little time we have to do so.

We can have a future-proof faith. We can have a faith that is not subject to the whims of a fast-changing culture or an increasingly hostile world. Our faith should stand up against all possible threats and remain steadfast and at peace in any and all circumstances. There is, however, nothing we can do to curtail the rising tides—those are beyond our ability to change.

The challenge of writing this book

Writing this book presented a serious challenge. The subject matter is so tied to current developments that I am constantly tempted to put off publication. Pulling the trigger to publish it is hard to do because new relevant information becomes available daily. How can I finish this book without including the latest newsworthy story? In fact, you will notice that most of the endnotes are links to online articles because much of the information is too current to find published in books.

The longer I wait to publish these thoughts, though, the more out-of-date all I have already written becomes. No matter when I pull that proverbial trigger, I will instantly miss some profound information and simultaneously solidify the impending irrelevance of other information that is included. The content of this book is of such importance that I simply must publish it sooner rather than later. So here it is. Read it now.

This book addresses things that are currently happening in our world. It is full of data that is relevant for right now—but not for long. No matter when you read these words, two things you can count on: things have progressed since the book's release and are probably worse then described, and we have even less time to make essential adjustments to face these challenges.

This book will need to be updated, or it will have a short shelf life. As such, I have an unusual request to make of you. If you think this information is significant, can I boldly ask that you tell others to read it before the book is out-of-date? Spread the word sooner, because later may be too late. Tell a friend.

This is not a doom and gloom book

This book contains a lot of alarming information, but it is not a "doom and gloom" book by any means. Fear is not my goal. Faith, hope, and love—the opposites of fear—are the intentions of this book. Do not lose sight of this as you read. Be sober minded, not fearful, as we face these exponential changes.

I admire futurists who look forward and bring to the present a picture of what may come. I, however, am not such a person. This is not a book about the future as much as it is about the now. This data is drawn from what currently is real. In a sense, that makes it more frightening, not less. Do not get stuck in the first part of the book, for there is hope and faith to be found in the latter half.

The more people who read this book and take it seriously, and the sooner they do so, the more prepared we can be as we face what has already arrived and will only get worse. Following the early chapters, which lay out the challenges we face, are solutions—real and viable solutions. Not solutions to the challenges themselves, but to our state of being and fruitfulness in the midst of them.

I will lay out possibilities that can help us catch up and keep up with these exponential changes and not be overtaken. The solutions are real, tangible, and doable, but making such changes will also be costly and hard. The pain involved with changing now will be far more palatable than the pain that will come if we do not make such changes. In fact, the longer we delay, the more pain we will face in changing. This is because the gap between where we are now and where we need to be in order to significantly impact this world is constantly growing wider.

Start paddling

I have lived my entire life near the ocean. My family has a history of surfing big waves—really big ones. I have risen and fallen on gigantic swells. I have been tossed around like a rag doll under the crushing force of waves that stand twenty feet tall before they crash.

As we rise on a growing swell, we can choose to look only at the water immediately surrounding us. When we do that, we do not feel like much has changed. But we can also choose to look over our shoulders and see how high on the crest we are. That's when the air leaves our lungs, all our muscles tense, and our eyes widen. This book is meant to help us see how high we are on the tip of a wave about to crash. We must decide to ride this wave or wipe out—those are the only choices. When our ears are popping from the altitude, it is time to start paddling.

Neil Cole
LONG BEACH, CALIFORNIA
MAY 2018

The Beginning of the End

*The ultimate measure of a man is not where he stands
in moments of comfort and convenience, but where he stands
at times of challenge and controversy.*
—Martin Luther King, Jr.

These are the times that try men's souls.
—Thomas Paine

IT WAS ON AN UNREMARKABLE SPRING AFTERNOON in 1980, in the third-floor lounge on the west wing of the Los Alamitos dormitory at California State University, Long Beach, when I naively surrendered my life to following Christ. That simple act would alter the entire trajectory of my life. All my days since then can trace their meaning to that one moment. It was undoubtedly the best decision I have ever made, and every decision since—both good and bad—is better because of it. I weighed the options for a year before I completed the spiritual transaction, so while it may have been naive, it was not without thought.

Coming from a home that was staunchly against Christianity, I didn't even know how much I didn't know. I was hungry to learn about Jesus. Unconnected to any church and without anyone to instruct me in the ways of Christ, I decided to start reading a Bible I received a few months earlier. When all else fails—or before—read the book.

I distinctly remember devouring the book of Acts for the very first time. I knew none of the stories. One morning I was unable to stop turning the pages, even though I was running out of time to get to my art class. Finally, I forced myself to shut the book, shoulder my backpack full of art supplies, and start jogging across campus.

With exciting stories fresh in my mind, I did something that I would now recognize as praying. I thought, "I wish I'd been alive back then to be a part of the story." In that moment, I clearly heard the voice of the Lord speaking to my soul for the first time. He interrupted my train of thought with an unexpected answer. It was full of love and wisdom—not audible, but clear. He said, "Those who lived then wish they were alive in these days."

These are significant times, ones of great change and unprecedented events. We cannot help but understand that these days are a culmination of all that has gone before and are gathering momentum toward a global breaking point. Stating the obvious, we are closer to the end than any who have gone before. Certainly we are closer to the second coming of Christ than we are to the first.

The apostle Paul said of Israel's former king, "David, after he had served the purpose of God in his own generation, fell asleep, and was laid among his fathers" (Acts 13:36). We are responsible for serving the purpose of God in our generation, and the challenge of this generation is unlike any before. Unfortunately, I meet many Christians who feel more responsible to previous generations and who are dropping the ball with the generation given to us.

While this book is an honest appraisal of the rising challenges the Church faces today and tomorrow, it is nonetheless a hopeful book. We plunge into a hostile future with some certainty and promise. Let me briefly share some positive truth to give us hope and courage.

Jesus said that the gates of hell will not prevail against the Church. Gates are not usually a threat, even if they are connected to hell itself. Gates are not made for offense but defense. The gate of a city in the Old Testament was the meeting place for the elders of that city. It was the brain trust where the powerful leaders of a city discussed important issues. The gates were also the final defense of the city.

All the strategic plotting and the powerful defenses of Satan and his horde are no match for Christ's Church. According to Jesus, we are to be on *offense*, and all the defenses of hell cannot prevent us from accomplishing our work. We step forward into the future with this promise. That is great news.

We are told in the twelfth chapter of the book of Hebrews:

> *For you have not come to a mountain that can be touched and to a blazing fire, and to darkness and gloom and whirlwind. [...] But you have come to Mount Zion and to the city of the living God, the heavenly Jerusalem, and to myriads of angels, to the general assembly and church of the firstborn who are enrolled in heaven, and to God, the Judge of all, and to the spirits of the righteous made perfect, and to Jesus, the mediator of a new covenant, and to the sprinkled blood, which speaks better than the blood of Abel.*
> HEBREWS 12:18, 22-24

Our fate is not one of terror and horror. We are called to something better, stronger, and eternal.

The passage then tells us that destruction not only happened in the days of the Old Testament but that it will also happen in the future:

> *but now He has promised, saying, "YET ONCE MORE I WILL SHAKE NOT ONLY THE EARTH, BUT ALSO THE HEAVEN." This expression, "Yet once more," denotes the removing of those things which can be shaken, as of created things, so that those things which cannot be shaken may remain.*
> HEBREWS 12:26-27

There is a shaking coming, and it will shake both the material world and the spiritual world at once. Only that which is unshakeable will remain. The writer continues:

> *Therefore, since we receive a kingdom which cannot be shaken, let us show gratitude, by which we may offer to God*

an acceptable service with reverence and awe; for our God is
a consuming fire.
HEBREWS 12:28-29

God promised us that the Church will prevail against hell itself, and the Kingdom of God cannot be shaken. That is good news in this rapidly changing world. I firmly believe that these days will experience a shaking unlike anything in history. We have hope—the true hope—in Christ and His Kingdom. But that needs to be our only hope if we want to remain standing. Hope in anything else will not endure.

Notice what the Bible doesn't say. It doesn't guarantee that your church meetings will continue. It doesn't promise that your Christian organization will be well funded. It doesn't state that your political party or national identity will win the culture war. God doesn't even promise that your family and prosperity will be untouchable—in fact, He says the opposite. We are not promised prosperity but persecution. We are not promised that we will win every cultural battle but rather that we will end up being hated just like our King. We are promised that everything that can be shaken will be shaken. Our problem is that much of our spiritual practice, and many of the props we count on, are highly shakeable.

Facing the exponential rise

Once there was a father who offered his two sons the choice of either one dollar a week for fifty-two weeks, or one cent the first week with the amount doubling the next week to just two cents but then continuing to double for fifty-two weeks. One son took the buck; the other took a chance and accepted the penny. We all know who wins. The son who took the dollar would have fifty-two dollars at the end of the year. The one who began with a penny would have enough money to pay off the US national debt by the end of the year—and still have plenty left over.

Multiplication is powerful. It hits that exponential growth curve and rockets to unfathomable numbers. There are four dramatic shifts occurring in our time that merit our immediate attention. These four areas are already high up the rising curve and only increasing in acceleration by the second. They demand that we think differently about who we are as Jesus' Church in these days.

If we want to fulfill the Great Commission, we must do things differently. "Church" as we have practiced it for centuries is shakeable; in fact, it's Jell-O. Our local church structures must shift to a more organic pattern that can *multiply* disciples rather than merely *add* people to the roster. This cannot simply be an option for some churches—we must change, or we will fall in the shaking like everything else in this world. The Church, as Jesus builds it, will prevail. Jesus' Kingdom is unshakeable. But as long as we put our confidence in our ecclesiastical structures and practices, we are fully shakeable, and hell will destroy what we have built.

PART ONE

Navigating the Now:
Four Trends of
Exponential Change

CHAPTER ONE

Too Many Rats in this Race: The Rising Population

*Our earth is becoming too small for us, global population is increasing at
an alarming rate, and we are in danger of self-destructing.*
—Stephen Hawking

The trouble with the rat race is that even if you win, you're still a rat.
—Lily Tomlin

THE CABIN LIGHTS FINALLY DIMMED on a red-eye flight as I was
returning home. Having been speaking all week, I was worn out and
just wanted to slide on headphones and an eye mask, lower my seat, and
forget the world for a few hours. The passenger next to me had other
plans. He was talkative. Reminding myself why I'm here on this planet
(and plane), I brushed aside my initial annoyance and engaged with him
enthusiastically, all the while praying for a meaningful conversation. It
was indeed memorable.

He was a Jewish doctor who sold medical equipment in Asia. He
asked me what I did, so I told him I was an author. Then he asked what
kind of books I wrote. I had the opportunity to tell him about myself and
what my life was about. I expected that to end the conversation—most
of the time it does. In this case, however, he was intrigued and wanted
to talk.

Somehow we began discussing the state of the world and whether
evil exists. The doctor believed that we were evolving to become better

humans and that evil was not inherent in us. He had recently read a book proving that we, as a species, are actually improving and evolving to become better.

"Really?" I asked. I brought up the Nazi Holocaust, Mao Zedong's slaughter of millions, Stalin's mass murders, the Khmer Rouge's killing fields, weekly terrorist attacks, and constant wars, and asked, "How does that sound like we are doing better than previous eras?" I commented, "The only thing we seem to be better at is killing more people with less effort or remorse than any previous generation."

His answer was that the population is much larger than previous generations, so the percentage of people being killed is actually much less than it used to be.

"How many people killed unnaturally would it take to prove that we are not getting better but worse?" I asked. He just looked at me. I could see that my odd question surprised him, and he was trying to figure out how to answer it. I added, "We already mentioned hundreds of millions, probably as many as a billion. How many killed, given our large population, would it take for us to be considered worse than any previous generation?"

I helped him out by saying, "If an additional billion lives were extinguished at the hands of other people during the last fifty years—above and beyond the other genocides already mentioned—would that be enough to destroy the hypothesis that we are better than the people of previous eras? That would put the unnatural death toll higher than 20 percent—would that be high enough?"

Nodding, the doctor answered, "Yes, an additional billion killings would probably change that argument." Then he added, "But it hasn't happened, so it's an irrelevant hypothetical question."

"Oh, but it has," I said. "Since 1970, there have been a billion abortions in the world. Our population would be a billion more if not for abortion. One billion lives have been extinguished by the hands of other people in less than fifty years." I then added, "That would bring the number of unnatural deaths due to genocide, war, and intentional eugenics up to about two billion in one hundred years, among a population that has grown from three to seven billion. Two billion killed, out of a potential nine billion lives—I would say that is a significant percentage of the total population. Are you still thinking that we are better than previous eras?"

Shaking his head he said, "Abortion doesn't count."

"I would say it counts," I retorted. "I'm glad I wasn't aborted. How about you? Are you glad you were allowed to live? Are you glad you were not aborted?"

He nodded. He had to. Quickly he went on to protest, "Yes, but…"

In the end, he refused to count those numbers. He preferred to believe that we are better people than previous humans. We had a lively debate and the time passed quickly, but I didn't change his mind and he didn't change mine. No one wants to believe they are worse than the people who were before them. We all want to think that we are the best. I get it. It is an unfortunate reality that many people would rather remain deluded than face the truth all around.

Lest you think that it is only the heathen and humanists of this world that are kidding themselves, we Christians are perhaps the most deluded. Our days are rapidly passing and time is no longer abundant. This is a wake-up call. We must abandon our old ways in order to become what we were always meant to be—a rapidly expanding, persecution-proof movement of Jesus' disciples.

A steep learning curve

We have heard the statistics about the population of our world. There are seven and a half billion souls living on this planet—and that number rises every second.

Having always lived during this population bloom, we may not realize how dramatic it is within the timeline of history. Perhaps a picture can help put context to our birthdays beyond candles and cake and demonstrate the consequence of being alive in these days.

Below is a chart to visualize the dramatic upswing we are in the midst of, shown from 10,000 BC until now.

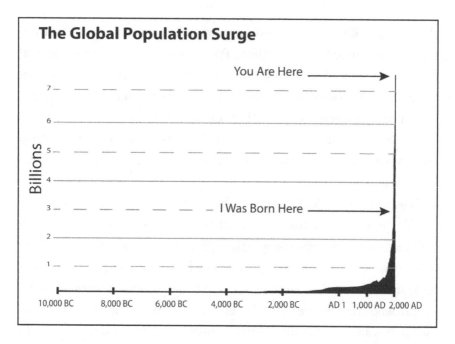

Figure 1.1

From the day Noah stepped off his boat, it took until 1804 AD to pass our first billion people living at once on this small blue planet. In just one century (1804–1900 AD), we tripled that number. In my lifetime we have grown by four billion—and I'm still breathing and tapping on these keys. How much higher could the spike rise during the rest of my life—or my children's lives?

Exponential growth is a powerful phenomenon. The momentum of this population growth has been a tidal wave hitting this planet. What could possibly slow it down? Plague? Wars? Economic collapse? Famine? Massive genocide? Weapons of mass destruction? Orchestrated eugenics? So far, these horrors have not slowed the pace.

If you were twenty years old in 1914, by the time you turned fifty you would have lived to see two world wars, the Nazi Holocaust, Stalin's great purge, two atomic bombs dropped on populated cities, the Great Depression, the Dustbowl and the Spanish Flu pandemic—and the momentum on the chart above never even paused for a moment. In fact, the rate of growth increased. Since 1970, there have been over a billion abortions globally. All of this devastation and unnatural loss of life has not even slowed the upswing of the growth curve. The momentum of exponential growth is something that is hard to fathom.

Whatever your view of the end times, you certainly have to agree that we are in significant days that are barreling toward a breaking point. Now consider that this is the era God chose to bring you into the world—you and seven and a half billion other souls (and counting).

The challenge of the task ahead of us

In the first century, Jesus gave His eleven surviving disciples a challenge. He said, "Go therefore and make disciples of all the nations" (Matthew 28:19). Can you imagine how impossible that sounded to a small group of fishermen, reformed tax collectors, and zealots? Well, it is nothing compared to the challenge He gives to you and me at this time. What was a few million is now a few billion, but the task has not changed. We must make immediate and drastic changes if we have any hope of fulfilling our call to make disciples of all the people groups.

Prior to the rise of Emperor Constantine, the more organic and movemental expression of the early Church succeeded in accomplishing what nothing else was able to do—defeat the Roman Empire in a head-to-head conflict. Rome considered this fledgling faith a challenge and did everything it could to stomp it out. In the end, the Empire surrendered to Christianity. For a brief moment, it seemed like the commission given to the Church by Jesus was fulfilled. But the old saying, "If you can't beat 'em, join 'em," was a strategy well played by the world. In no time, Christianity was overcome—not by brute force, but by the seduction of power and privilege. Under Emperor Constantine, Christianity not only became legal, but worse, profitable. The Church became a political enterprise, with all that entails. The Constantinian expression of church was born.

What is the Constantinian model of church? It is what comes to your mind when you ask yourself, "What is a local church?" It is a location, often a building, where clergy conduct sacred activities on special days for the faithful in attendance. As common as that understanding is to us, it is actually foreign to the New Testament.

This model that came into prominence post-Constantine was not sufficiently able to make disciples of the world even when the population was a fraction of what it is today. The Constantinian model of church has remained in place since the 300s AD. The global population back then was about the size of the current US population, but the Church failed to fulfill the Great Commission. In order to reach this world, we have no other option then to consider "organizing" under a different paradigm, that releases multiplication so that we can fulfill the commission given to us by Jesus.

Unfortunately, church leaders invest everything they have in making that ineffective model work. Why? Because their security, identity, and purpose are intertwined with that model's function. Those who have the best opportunity to make it change are the very people most motivated to keep it the same. As Upton Sinclair once quipped, "It is difficult to get a man to understand something, when his salary depends upon his not understanding it!"[1] Our leadership is invested in upholding a model that is incapable of accomplishing what God asks of it. This model has been in place for one and a half millennia, so it now has become our very definition of church. It is a challenge to imagine anything else, but we must if we are to make a difference in this generation.

A final word on the "rat race"

I would be remiss if I did not mention that in recent days the pace of exponential growth of the population appears to be slowing. While violent force could not slow the growth, other factors seem to be more effective at doing so in our modern world. Education, economics, modern medicine, and selfishness are decreasing the birthrate.[2]

There is much speculation about whether the population will grow, slow, plateau, or even subside in the future. What is not under debate is the incredible exponential growth rate we have already experienced, illustrated in the diagram above. It is clear that our current means of doing church and reaching the world are inadequate. Remember, this book is about the now, not the future. We can debate the future, but no one disputes the exponential growth rate of the population and where we are now in terms of billions.

If the population growth were the only rapid current we need to deal with, it would be enough to challenge our church structures—but it is not. In the following chapters I will lay out for you three other exponential swings upward that set the stage for the Church to either fade into irrelevance or rise to the challenge of our times.

CHAPTER TWO

The Skynet is Falling:
The Rising Technology Tsunami

In the last few years, we've moved from an information-scarce economy to one driven by an information glut. According to Eric Schmidt of Google, every two days we create as much information as we did from the dawn of civilization until 2003. That's about five exobytes of data a day, for those of you keeping score. The challenge becomes, not finding that scarce plant growing in the desert, but finding a specific plant growing in a jungle. We are going to need help navigating that information to find the thing we actually need.
—Neil Gaiman

Any sufficiently advanced technology is indistinguishable from magic.
—Arthur C. Clarke

IN 2016, I WAS INVITED to share at an elite conference on technology. Elon Musk, Bill Gates, and many powerful innovators, entrepreneurs, and world changers were addressing the audience. This was an invitation-only event, and the tickets cost thousands of dollars, which I could never afford. I was invited to come and share, so I didn't have to pay. What would I have to share at such a prestigious event? Coffee. I was there as an anonymous barista serving coffee to those in attendance.

I was able to hear all the keynote presentations for free—well, for service. A surprisingly common belief shared by the speakers was that we are rapidly approaching what experts call a *singularity*—one single event that will change everything as we now know it. They expect a technological "event horizon" beyond which our human imaginations can't even fathom. Think androids, immortality, and interstellar travel.

Futurist author Ray Kurzweil predicts that this singularity will occur specifically in 2045. "We won't experience 100 years of progress in the 21st century—it will be more like 20,000 years of progress (at today's rate)," wrote Kurzweil in 2001.[1] He bases much of his forecast on the exponential growth rate of technology.

Kurzweil notes, "When I was an undergraduate, we all shared a computer at MIT that took up half of a building. The computer in your cellphone today is a million times cheaper and a thousand times more powerful. That's a billion fold increase in price performance of computing since I was an undergraduate."[2]

Most expect the singularity to be the birth of true artificial (or advanced) intelligence (AI), where created intelligence can not only think and solve problems, but also learn and develop its own self-awareness and independent decision-making. Experts expect this advancement will launch humanity into a giant evolutionary step forward.[3] Technology and biology will merge to create a new breed of humanity. In their thinking, we will become better than human and will never go back to mere mortality.

Every year, computers become faster at computations and more able to interact with humans in subtle, intuitive, and personable ways. First we heard that computers could beat people in checkers. Later they beat us in chess. At the time I am writing this (February 2017), computers were able to beat five of the world's best professional poker players.[4] That is a little scary because one must be intentionally deceptive to win at poker. Can a computer bluff? Apparently so, and better than a human.

The race to AI is not science fiction. Robotics and AI are rapidly developing industries. All the biggest tech companies are buying up research in this area. Google's founder, Larry Page, hired Kurzweil to oversee the development of AI. They also bought several AI and robotics companies.[5] Smart and hugely successful people don't just believe this; they are investing all they have in it…and will make it happen. It is coming faster than we imagine. And it will reach a tipping point that changes everything as we know it.

Not everyone in the know is flippant about our progress in this field. In fact, some of our most intelligent and successful people are warning us that we need to get ahead of this thing before it is too late. Bill Gates[6], Elon Musk, and the late Stephen Hawking,[7] have all warned us of a coming existential threat via artificial intelligence. If you were tasked to come up with three people with the mental acuity to express such a concern, it would likely be the list above. Each of them have virtually voiced the same thing: "I don't understand why some people are not concerned."[8]

Elon Musk has access to technological advances we do not. In July 2017, he said to the National Governors Association summer meeting:

> I have exposure to the very cutting edge AI, and I think people should be really concerned about it. I keep sounding the alarm bell, but until people see robots going down the street killing people, they don't know how to react, because it seems so ethereal. [...]AI is a rare case where we need to be proactive about regulation instead of reactive [...] by the time we are reactive in AI regulation, it's too late.[9]

He speculates the chances of creating a safe AI at only 5-10 percent.[10] That's a 90-95 percent chance of AI being dangerous to humanity's well-being and existence.[11]

With dollar signs in our eyes and convenience in our minds, we are moving at warp speed toward a future with reckless abandon and little restraint. But this chapter is not as much about where things will go in the near future as much as where we are presently.

The 300,000 mph VW Bug

Gordon Moore (co-founder of Intel) predicted in 1965 that the computer processor would double in capacity and speed every year for the next decade. Ten years later, he stated it would double every two years. While there have been natural fluctuations in the rate, his predictions have proven accurate enough that this is called *Moore's Law*. It states that the computer chip will double in capacity and speed every twenty-four months, which produces an exponential rate of advancement in computer power.[12]

Exponential growth is difficult for people to comprehend. To demonstrate how reliable Moore's prediction has been, consider the increase in the advance of computer processing of Intel's own processors. Intel's first-generation microchip from 1971 (the 4004) compared against Intel's sixth-generation Intel Core processor reveals that Intel's newer chip offered 3,500 times more performance, is 90,000 times more energy efficient, and is about 60,000 times lower in cost. And by the time this is published, they will have likely doubled or quadrupled those figures.

To help us understand the power of this growth, Brian Krzanich, Intel's CEO, uses the following analogy (as explained in Thomas L. Friedman's book *Thank You For Being Late*):

> *Intel engineers did a rough calculation of what would happen had a 1971 Volkswagen Beetle improved at the same rate as microchips did under Moore's law. These are the numbers: Today, that Beetle would be able to go about three hundred thousand miles per hour. It would get two million miles per gallon of gas, and it would cost four cents! Intel engineers also estimated that if automobile fuel efficiency improved at the same rate as Moore's law, you could, roughly speaking, drive a car your whole life on one tank of gasoline.[13]*

Moore's Law is not really a law, but more of a prediction based on his observations. In the beginning, the rate was doubling every twelve months. At one point, computer processing was doubling at an eighteen-month rate. Some speculate that the pace stated in Moore's Law is slowing down, and capacity is now doubling about every thirty months. Moore himself has predicted that the law will die in the next decade.[14]

Doubling every two years or every four years is still an exponential rate of growth to reckon with. What likely occurs is that the rate slows just before a huge breakthrough that will jump-start the rate once again. Currently, researchers are working to develop a neural network for processing data that mimics the process of the brain rather than the hardware we are accustomed to.[15] Who knows what revolutionary breakthrough will come about before you even finish reading this chapter?

My wife teaches pre-kindergarten special education in Los Angeles, working with kids with special needs. Many are unable to talk, walk, or even feed themselves, but they can swipe their way around a tablet with ease. People from my generation view the tablet and smartphone as new advancements that are helpful tools. This next generation and the one to follow will not remember life without them—in fact, they will probably soon come to view them as antiques.

When our children grow up in our home, they can be on a rapid growth spurt, and we may not notice. If not for the notches on the kitchen doorframe (and receipts for new shoes every couple months), we would see them each day as the same—but they are not. If we were separated for a few years and then reunited, we would be shocked to see how much they had grown. I believe we are not noticing how much technology is affecting our lives, simply because we live each day with what is happening and fail to gain a long-range view.

I was traveling about one hundred miles to a secluded spot for a writing retreat, hoping to finish this book. There is nothing new about that; authors have been doing that for hundreds of years. Nevertheless, we take for granted being able to travel one hundred miles in just over an hour.

But that is only a fraction of what made this trip remarkable. I was also on a video conference call the entire drive with three other team members, discussing the maturation process of church systems. One of us was in Denver, another in Virginia, and the third in Copenhagen, while I was in the Los Angeles basin. That is still not very remarkable these days, but when you look at it historically, it is amazing.

At the same time, however, a prerecorded interview of me was being broadcast by a radio program in Minnesota. There were preloaded tweets quoting me from the interview that were scheduled to hit the Internet as I was speaking on the air. All of this was occurring while I was on a conference call and driving at over sixty miles per hour on a California freeway.

You may not be at all impressed with what took place in that hour. All this does not feel like a new breakthrough in technology, but just a few years ago this would have been an impossible dream. From the perspective of a person driving on a highway in St. Paul, I was talking with the radio host and tweeting quotes from it simultaneously. The truth is that the host was on vacation, I was on a conference call, the show was prerecorded, and the tweets were scheduled several hours prior, to coincide with the show.

Four ways rapid tech innovation is changing our lives

Those who follow Christ must consider themselves missionaries to this world, and as such, we need a better understanding of the forces that shape society. Here are four important ways that life-as-we-know-it is changing rapidly due to technology.

1. Language: What took a few centuries now morphs in a few years

Sharon Downey, a university professor of mine, one day opened class with the statement: "If you want to change a culture, change its language."[16] Our language is changing faster than at any other time in history. It seems like every year we have a whole new dictionary of words to learn. New verbs are created weekly. It is perfectly legal to Google, text, tweet, Skype, Instagram, Snapchat, hashtag, swipe, and Wiki people as often as you want, as long as we don't "sext" them without permission. Webster needs to add a whole new definition to what it means to "like" a "friend."

We can "Uber" to places but we can't "flash drive" anywhere. We can "surf the web" and "search" for the perfect wave and never leave our basement. We can put "software" on our "hardware" and get "malware" from "shareware" in our "gameware" and do it all in our underwear—from anywhere. We can "tweet" and "retweet" people's "comments" to all our "followers" and post it on our "blog" with a "link" to our "Facebook" "home page".

Most people understand what I've written in the paragraph above, but we would not have understood it just twenty years ago. Imagine what C.S. Lewis or J.R.R. Tolkien would think of that paragraph if they read it in their lifetime. *Is that an ancient elvish tongue you speak?* Like me trying to read Shakespeare in high school, they would recognize almost every word and understand few of them.

With texting, and the limitation of 140 characters in the twittersphere, we now communicate without complete words. Conventional slang abbreviation has its own dictionary. Sometimes we use numbers instead of words, and punctuation is now superfluous. We use a bunch of letters to say what used to be complete sentences: Ip lol html url bff btw brb cya imho irl np gr8 l8r omg pov rotflmao thx stby tmi. Just a few years ago, that list of letters and numbers would appear as some random typing from a chimpanzee. Today, any person under thirty will likely know what each set of characters means—yet they may have difficulty writing with decent grammar and suffer from a diminished vocabulary. "If people cannot write well, they cannot think well," said George Orwell. He added, "And if they cannot think well, others will do the thinking for them."[17] Welcome to today.

We are too close to see how fast this is all happening. What took four centuries for Macbeth to lose in translation is now happening in half a decade because of the pop-digital world and technological advancement.

2. Tech-dependence: We are tied to our tools and can't think or act without them

Innovation can change the world. This is not a surprise. When footwear was invented and improved, Alexander conquered the world, seemingly over-night. Rome invented the road and ruled the globe for a thousand years. A man invented a printing press, and civilization was changed for centuries to follow. These world-altering innovations occurred with centuries, even millennia, between. Today, such breakthroughs are occurring almost annually.

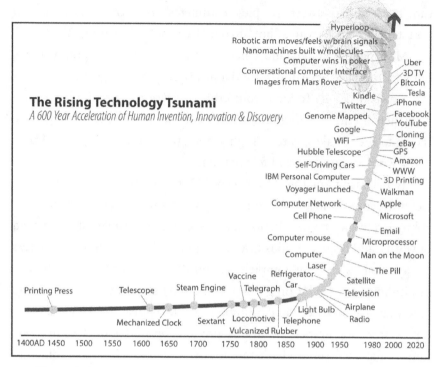

Figure 2.1

Currently, scientific data output increases by 30 percent annually. That means that the total scientific output doubles every three to four years.[18] This is far up the exponential growth curve and rising rapidly.

We've become so dependent on smartphones that when we lose a mobile phone, we feel like life might come to a grinding halt. It is not just inconvenient; when we lose our mobile phone, it is almost considered dangerous.

On a recent trip, I got to airport security and realized I had left my phone at home. I felt a deep sense of panic. Then my mind began to rehearse all the options I had—buying a new phone when I landed (but not having my contacts), having my phone shipped with next day air, etc. Instead, I merely borrowed the phone of the person behind me in line, called my son, and had him deliver my phone to me at the airport curb in time to catch my flight. It was close, and I had to go through security twice, but I felt twice as secure with my phone in my pocket. The thought of going two weeks without a phone was impossible to accept.

Think about that. Life for tens of thousands of years went forward without even imagining such a device, and now one day without it is viewed as *dangerous.*

My friend Alex Absalom wrote, "It's funny how the more resources we have, the less resourceful we tend to become."[19] We have all this technology and are instantly and constantly in touch, but we are not relating as deeply as we once did. We are also incapable of being all there wherever we are.

I had a flight delayed at O'Hare Airport in Chicago. In the gate area were over one hundred people seated in every available chair. I stood in the midst of all these people and noticed that every single person within my view, without exception, had a phone in his or her hands absorbing all their attention. No one was talking to anyone—though they could have been texting the person sitting next to them. It was so astonishing that I got out my phone and took a picture and posted it on Instagram with a snarky comment. In that moment I realized I too had a phone in my hand absorbing my attention.

We are losing life skills as quickly as we are gaining technical tools. Advancing scientific discovery and technology is usually greeted with fear and insecurity by the Church. The Church universal, however, has always benefitted from technological advancement. Paul used the Roman roads to reach the world. The printing press set God's Word free to impact the masses.

A tool is neither evil nor good; it has no moral or spiritual quality whatsoever. It is the heart of the person that uses it that can be either helpful or hurtful. A hammer can be used to crush a skull or build a bridge. The hammer carries no blame for how it is used. It is not inherently evil or righteous. We cannot "save" a hammer; it has no soul. There is no Christian tool, nor secular tool—there is just the tool in the hands of someone ruled by Christ or not.

With a smartphone we now have instant access to all human

knowledge at our fingertips—literally. I have access to hundreds of translations of the Bible with a dictionary and encyclopedia of Bible facts in my front pocket 24/7. Imagine what the apostle Paul could do today with air travel, translation apps, Bible translations, and other communication tools. It is daunting to think what he could do with all that we are blessed with, yet none of us have seen the world changed as much as he did in a single short life. It is not the tool's fault. We are the people with a hammer in our hands; let's build something good.

3. Laws: Courts cannot keep up and will never catch up

"The rate of technological change is now accelerating so fast that it has risen above the average rate at which most people can absorb all these changes. Many of us cannot keep pace anymore."[20] Nowhere is this dilemma more pressing than in our legal system.

Eric Teller, the CEO of Google's X research and development lab, which produced Google's self-driving car says the following:

> In the decades following the invention of the internal combustion engine—before the streets were flooded with mass-produced cars—traffic laws and conventions were gradually put into place. Many of those laws and conventions continue to serve us well today, and over the course of a century, we had plenty of time to adapt our laws to new inventions, such as freeways. Today, however, scientific advances are bringing seismic shifts to the ways in which we use our roads; legislatures and municipalities are scrambling to keep up, tech companies are chafing under outdated and sometimes nonsensical rules, and the public is not sure what to think. Smartphone technology gave rise to Uber, but before the world figures out how to regulate ride-sharing, self-driving cars will have made those regulations obsolete.[21]

Laws and governments cannot keep pace with the increase of technology. When you buy the latest smartphone, another breakthrough makes it out-of-date in the time you took charging the battery the first time. Copyright, patent, intellectual property, and ownership protocols are constantly being rewritten—and become superseded before the ink dries. What can you do to protect your creation if it takes four to five years to secure a patent, but your technological innovation becomes obsolete in half that time?

In fact, technology actually develops much faster than it is released to the consumer because of the need for corporations (and the government) to make as much profit off the previous generation of tech before the next one is released. It is bad business to release technology too quickly—the companies have to pay for the research and development that created it and then make a sizeable profit before they let it go out-of-date.

We now live in a time when leading businesses can thrive without any products or property. Tom Goodwin, senior vice president of strategy and innovation at Havas Media, observed:

> Uber, the world's largest taxi company, owns no vehicles. Facebook, the world's most popular media owner, creates no content. Alibaba, the most valuable retailer, has no inventory. And Airbnb, the world's largest accommodation provider, owns no real estate. Something interesting is happening.[22]

The artistic industries are one area where the rapid innovation affecting ownership and rights of authorship is most evident. It is no secret that technological breakthroughs are benefitting our creativity, such as CGI in cinema and the rise in independent artists in literature, music, and film. That is good news to most artists, who can see this as a new renaissance of creativity. However, there is also a dark side to this technological advance.

It is increasingly hard to make a living in the arts. This was first felt in the music industry where people found they could download songs for free on the Internet with Napster and other illegal shareware. These small businesses were sued by the big five music companies and lost the suits…all of them. Before the big companies won a single lawsuit, however, they lost the war, because the audience had a taste for free music and would no longer tolerate paying for it. Today, artists are looking for ways to make a living from music, and the options are quickly evaporating. The audience expects music for free or very cheap.

In the process, the art has been cheapened, and the process of creating has lost its payoff. The result will be increasing mediocrity in music. Creative artists will still produce—they can't help it. But the means to getting that music out in such a way that the creators can make a living by it is evaporating. When art becomes only a hobby, it cannot be as creative or revolutionary.

This is also happening in the world of literature. Now it is cheap and easy for anyone to publish a book, and the independent publishing world is on the rise. But like the musicians, authors find it more and more challenging to make a living by writing books, as the audience is getting accustomed to acquiring books for minimal to no cost.

Globalization is on the rise, and pirating books, films, and music is commonplace in many nations of the world; selling the stolen product cheaply online to every nation is prolific. It is impossible to enforce the laws written in one nation upon another. Even if they could, by the time they fix the law, another boom in technology would have everyone getting their book, film, or music for free at another source. No matter how speedy we attempt to be in our courts, our laws simply cannot be passed by Congress fast enough to legislate the behavior of the global audience consuming the art.

Perhaps the most startling area where laws cannot keep pace with technological advancement is in the collection and use of data. This is such a striking development that it merits its own category in the discussion.

4. Surveillance: Data mining, profiling, predicting and targeting

We have shifted from the information age to the surveillance age, and we made that shift willingly, with little awareness of what was truly happening. We just upgraded our smartphones, pressed the "I Accept" button to three pages of fine print legalese that none of us read, and instantly we were feeding our information to companies that would sell it to others.

The collection of data is now so easy that it doesn't require a person to collect it, categorize it, or store it; computers do that automatically and without needing a paycheck or so much as a coffee break.

There is a false sense of security in the anonymity of being in a world saturated with data. We feel safe, thinking all the data from all the people allows us to remain unnoticed in it all. How could all that information actually be meaningful to anyone? We think no one can possibly notice us in the midst of this ever-expanding universe of minutiae called "big data." But the belief that our information is lost in an endless ocean of unimportant data is just not true.

Technology has shifted there as well. Algorithms and computer processing has enabled large corporations to know the tiniest details of our lives and compose virtual yet three-dimensional pictures of us. Using algorithmic projections, these programs can accurately predict behavior, preferences, and outcomes. This is what Cambridge Analytica was doing with data mined from Facebook to sway voters.[23] A person doesn't do this—the computer itself knows all about us—but people can use that information, for or against us.

Every day, we create 2.5 quintillion bytes of data. "Quintillion" is a word beyond our ability to comprehend. Let me help. Ninety percent of all the data amassed in the world today has been created in the last two years alone. This data comes from everywhere: sensors used to gather climate information, posts to social media sites, digital pictures and videos, everything viewed on your smartphone or computer, every movie or television show viewed, purchase transaction records, and cell phone GPS signals, to name a few. This is called big data.[24] Internet-based companies are awash with data that can be analyzed and utilized by machines. Is this a good thing?[25]

Big data is a big deal. Big data is also big money. Marketing is tailored and sent our way instantly. It always bothers me when I simply browse for an item on a virtual storefront such as Amazon.com and find that for weeks those same items appear as ads on every page I open and each email I read or write. No human is doing that—it is all done with the programs running through the computer servers. But that is just the tip of the iceberg when we start to imagine what is possible with such information.

Every swipe of our fingers and every tap on our keyboards gives information to hidden industries. We all know this. But still it goes on. The industries used to get a slap on the wrist and a wink, along with a fine that was a fraction of the profit they made. The next day they would just do it again. In fact, they were incentivized to do it more. These small fines were merely the cost of doing business. But even those fines are now being brushed aside.

The US Senate recently voted to make it perfectly legal for a corporation to collect our data and sell our web browsing history without our permission.[26] Let this idea sink in. We feel like we are free in this country to choose to act anyway we want, but in some cases, our activity is no longer ours. Our government just decided that records of our activity (browsing, viewing, searching, sending, purchasing, commenting, liking, reviewing, reading, etc.) don't belong to us. They are now owned by a corporation and can be sold and/or used for their profit. Not only do they not need our permission, we don't get paid for the service we provide. We also have no means to refuse to participate. This is not just an attack on our privacy and freedom. It is a business that is built on using us without recompense.

They know where we go and what we like and dislike, both literally and virtually. They know how we like our coffee and what kind of underwear we prefer. They know our shopping habits and health issues. Our voting and entertainment preferences are all part of the virtual composite of us found in big data, which corporations own and the government accesses.

In the end, we may be known better by the intelligence behind all this than by our own spouses, parents, or children. Elon Musk warns,

"Facebook, Google, and Amazon [...] have more information about you than you can remember. There's a lot of risk in concentration of power. So if AGI [artificial general intelligence] represents an extreme level of power, should that be controlled by a few people at Google with no oversight?"[27] The question we need to ask ourselves is: do we think the people behind this have our best interests at heart, or could this end up hurting us?

We know that the government and big corporations are tracking us on our phones.[28] They can turn on the mic and record us even when the phone appears to not be on.[29] Edward Snowden warned us all of this ability.[30] Our government criminalizes the whistle-blowers who leak this information to us. Does that bother you?

Contrary to early campaign rhetoric, the rate of surveillance rose exponentially in many key areas under the Obama administration, including information gathered from telephone, email, and other Internet communications. This was made evident in documents released by the Department of Justice (DOJ), following a Freedom of Information Act request by the American Civil Liberties Union.[31] In the short amount of time that Donald Trump has been president, the laws allowing companies to profit from big data have loosened even more.

Addressing the mining of our electronic lives, Barack Obama said, "You can't have 100 percent security and also then have 100 percent privacy and zero inconvenience. We're going to have to make some choices as a society." We have sacrificed our privacy for the mythological promise of security and the convenience of online shopping. Now none of us feel any more secure, and we are only beginning to awaken to how much our convenient lifestyle is costing us in freedom and privacy.

The assurance offered to us was, "Nobody is listening to your telephone calls."[32] In most cases it is true that there is no "body" on the other end of the line listening in on our calls or reading our texts and email.[33] It is a computer that is listening, collecting, analyzing, and sometimes flagging the information—not a person. A person will not have cause to look at it unless something deemed to be nefarious is flagged. This, however, does not satisfy concerns about privacy and freedom in this surveillance age.

There are many myths perpetuated to give us a false sense of peace about this.[34] We have been led to believe that the computer is only searching for volatile words such as "jihad," but that is not how the system works. The algorithm is far more powerful than that and is organizing all the data on all of us, and especially now that "big data" is for sale to the highest bidder. This is not simply a way to catch terrorists and keep us all safer.

Do not be so foolish as to think this is a partisan issue either. When George Bush pushed the legal envelope of surveillance, it set up Obama to use the lenience allowed. When Obama extended the surveillance laws, he set a new precedent for Trump to use. Even if we trust one side of the political aisle, that doesn't matter, because the other side of the aisle will have the same leverage or more in just a few years. This is an individual privacy issue, not a political one.

This is not hidden in a hangar at Area 51 in some grand conspiracy theory. This is not science fiction; it is fact. We have recorded cases of such things all the time, publicly reported. We just blindly go about our lives thinking that the government and big businesses are not really malevolent.

The fragile protection that people of faith once had in anonymity and remaining underground during the reign of hostile regimes is gone forever. The government will no longer have to rely upon neighbors and family members turning us in—we do it ourselves. There is no longer a need for spies to infiltrate; we are now broadcasting our whereabouts, activities, beliefs, and relationships for the world to see. And the world is not any more benevolent or neutral than at other times in history. Under the banner of "Peace and Safety," our freedoms and privacy are being stolen.

Remember, I am not writing to offer any solutions to these rapidly rising tides. Better people than I will be needed for that. I remind you that the purpose of this book is to raise awareness of realities around us and then to help us to gain perspective and a foothold for proactive faith in the midst of them.

These are the days we are in, and I am afraid we are woefully unprepared for them. While this is happening, a few people are seizing the majority of power in this world. That is the next item for our discussion.

CHAPTER THREE

Stuck in the (Shrinking) Middle with You: The Rising Economic Gap

The future is already here—it's just not very evenly distributed.
—William Gibson

That's why they call it the American Dream,
because you have to be asleep to believe it.
—George Carlin

THAT THERE ARE DIFFERENT LEVELS OF WEALTH is not news at all. In fact, that truth is as old as dirt and wouldn't merit discussion in this book. What is alarming, is that the gap between each level is now widening at an ever-increasing rate. The extremely wealthy are rapidly becoming richer, and the middle class is deteriorating at the same pace.

The growing economic divide

At the risk of sounding like Bernie Sanders' campaign manager, I believe we are in the midst of a historic shift of wealth and power to a select few. Some chide Sanders for proposing a redistribution of wealth, but we are already experiencing the largest redistribution of wealth in human history.

Since the economic crisis of 2008/9, the number of billionaires has doubled from 793 to 1645.[1] Does that surprise you? While the rest of us ride the ups and downs of elevated joblessness, shrinking paychecks, increasing debt, decreasing value of our currency, the rising cost of living, and the depreciation of our property, there has been a steady upswing in the number of incredibly rich people. The wealthy ride out economic swings better than the rest of us, and when they suffer a setback, our government bails them out with our taxes. In the economic system of the last few years, the government provides assistance to the very rich and the very poor. Who pays for that assistance? Those in the middle.

The number of those whose financial status is falling are multiplying. Last year the dwindling middle class[2] was no longer the majority in the US.[3] There are more people in poverty and wealth combined than there are in between. The wealth is being redistributed, and we are powerless to do anything about it. The middle-income households are defined as those whose real incomes are within 50 to 150 percent of the median income. Households with incomes below this range are viewed as low income and above it, high income.

Income polarization in the United States has seen a significant increase since the 1970s. According to an Allianz report, the US is at the top of the list when calculating inequality ratios. "The U.S. had the most wealth inequality [...] showing the most concentration of overall wealth in the hands of the proportionately fewest people."[4] At the time of this writing, eight individuals have the combined wealth of half the world's population.[5]

One of the richest men in the world, Bill Gates, can't give his money away fast enough to slow down the increase. Since 2006, when he declared his departure from Microsoft, his wealth has grown by 50 percent or $25 billion.[6] In 2017, the wealthiest people on earth increased their wealth by $237 billion that year.[7]

The eighty-five richest people in the world increase their wealth by $688 million per day. That's $500,000/min. or $30 million an hour.[8] What is more unfathomable then gaining that kind of wealth is trying to figure out how to spend that much money. Breaking even becomes impossible.

Imagine trying to spend $30 million in one hour. Then imagine having to do the same thing again the next hour. At some point you already own everything, and yet you just made another $30 million and then another and another. For what?

This is more than financial greed. In fact, this passed greed a long time ago. This is about something else. It is a grasp at power and nothing less than a desire to own and rule the world. Does that sound paranoid to you?

When you are that rich and can buy anything you want anytime you want it and only see your accounts increase by almost a billion dollars that same day, soon you begin to think anything is possible. "I can own anything, anyone or even…everything and everyone." You might even decide on a whim to run for president of the United States. But why would you? The insanely rich already have far more power than any office can afford. In fact, they likely own many of the politicians in office already. This has been happening under the political watch of both parties. Both sides of the aisle are guilty of this redistribution of wealth and pointing their fingers at the other side.

Wealth building can happen from baking more pies via innovation and entrepreneurial enterprise, or by scrambling to hoard what remains of an existing pie. Both means create wealthy people and grant them power, but only one of them lifts and benefits society as a whole. The other enslaves the masses by diminishing their worth and forcing them to work harder for less.

We are seeing a few take as much as they can from wherever they can get it. I do not advocate socialism or communism—those experiments have failed enough to discount them. I do advocate that some restraint be placed on greed by just enforcing laws already in existence and perhaps legislating some fairer laws. We would need more courageous legislators to pull that off.

Taking wealth from the future

There is a simplistic distinction between the two sides of the debate (conservative and progressive). The liberal/progressive side (that leans toward socialism) views wealth as a limited commodity that needs to be stewarded with equity. The conservative side views wealth as having the potential to grow and multiply. Okay, I said it was simplistic.

Both sides, however, are adopting policies that have virtually identical results—increasing the national debt, increasing the wealth of the super rich, and reducing the financial stability of the middle class. While the few are becoming ever richer, the US debt is increasing to unfathomable proportions. It is not enough that these powerful elites are taking money from us; they are also seizing it from our children's future—and their children's.

Our grandparents owned homes and had a pension on only one income. Today, few can afford that. It is necessary for most families to have two incomes to own a home. Pensions are no longer routinely offered by employers. Employees need to take responsibility for preparing for their retirement, but they are too busy working two jobs to pay the bills due today to worry about the bills that are coming ten or twenty years from now. Our children may not be able to own a home with only two incomes. There isn't a single state in the US where a full-time job with a minimum wage is sufficient to even rent a two-bedroom apartment today.[9]

While I was writing this book, the US national debt topped twenty trillion dollars for the first time.[10] To pay debts today, the government has started to just print more money. Currency that is not tied to an actual asset, but only tied to the confidence of its people, will be as strong as the paper it is made of when the rain of people's fear and insecurity starts to pour down. Suddenly we find ourselves in an environment where the government and media must spin things in certain ways just to maintain the fragile confidence of people, in order to continue the system as is and not have it crash and burn.

Taking wealth from the middle

If you think I am overstating the economic situation, you have not been paying attention. The US government, under both Republican George Bush and Democrat Barack Obama has bailed out many of the largest companies by giving them your tax money. The list of companies bailed out is extensive and includes many well-known corporations.[11]

Initially, people were led to believe that the federal government bailed out big banks and corporations to the tune of $700 billion. That alone is astonishing, but it's not near as shocking as the real truth of it. The bailout has continued—that first $700 billion was just the initial payment. According to a summary by the inspector general of the Troubled Asset Relief Program (TARP), the total commitment of our government to bail out these huge corporations is closer to $15 trillion. More than $4.5 trillion has already been paid out, making the initial $700 billion seem like a drop in the ocean.[12]

Think about that. Where does the government get the money to pay for the mistakes of wealthy companies that are "too big to fail"? When large corporations become richer quicker by putting more people in debt and then find the loans they are giving out are failing, the rich companies that broke and bent laws to gain quick wealth do not pay for their mistakes, taxpayers and homeowners do.

For the first time in history, a majority of the members of the United States Congress are millionaires. Those in the Senate have an average net worth of $2.9 million.[13] It is extremely rare to find a US Representative who is not at least a millionaire, and it's quite common to find multimillionaires. They are supposedly our civil servants, but that is not how things work these days. There is not any real representation of the middle class in our government, even though the middle class carries much of the weight of its government. "The most perfect political community," Aristotle said, "is one in which the middle class is in control, and outnumbers both of the other classes." That once described the United States of America, but no longer.

Wealth wants to rule over us

You may state that this is all a very simplistic summary of complex issues, and you would be right. The intent of this book is not to solve the complexities of these issues but simply to state their reality and our need to fulfill our calling in the midst of them. I merely want to get us to the place where we can be fruitful and multiply people of good news during these challenging times. So don't consider this a treatise on economics as much as a description of the financial world we have to deal with today.

Those of us working in Christian ministry face increasing challenges. The more our ministries are dependent on this system to survive, the easier it will be for "the god of this world" to pull the rug right out from under us. If we are putting our hope in a political agenda to reform our economic system, we are guilty of idolatry. Fixing these problems is not our job—it never was. Financial security is not the goal of our faith. Nationalism and political partisanship is a distraction from what we are actually put on this earth to do. If we believe more money will increase the Kingdom, we have not studied the Gospels.

What is money anyway? Have you ever really asked that? Is money only paper with ink printed on it? No. It is the confidence we put in what that paper represents. We are quickly advancing into a cashless society where money is just confidence in a system—one that is bent and broken. Wealth is actually more than just a lot of money. It is a means of power and influence as well as the accumulation of things.

Jesus personified true wealth. He didn't speak of lust or hatred as if those temptations had their own personalities, but He did speak that way of wealth. In a very real sense, wealth has a personality and a will of its own—it is a spirit. I realize that sounds crazy, but Jesus spoke of it that way.

The word Jesus used to describe this spirit is "mammon." He stated boldly that, "No one can serve two masters; for either he will hate the one and love the other, or he will be devoted to one and despise the other. You cannot serve God and wealth [mammon]" (Matthew 6:24). Wealth seems to have intent and a will that we can serve. It is deceptive (Matthew 13:22). Those surrendered to it as a master are deceived and a slave to malicious intentions.

Wealth and Jesus are in a very real conflict over the souls and wills of human beings. Each is fighting against the other. Let that sink in. Those who are serving wealth, and whom wealth is blessing in return, will not be in favor of Jesus or His people.

Is it possible for someone who has great material wealth to not serve mammon? Yes, but it is only possible by God's miraculous grace. Jesus said it is easier for a camel to go through the eye of a needle than a rich man to enter God's Kingdom (Matthew 19:24). It is impossible for people—but not for God. He has done this miracle many times throughout history, but it is nonetheless a rare occurrence. Those with great wealth that do come under the reign of God's Kingdom frequently end up dying with little money but great peace and joy.

If the greed and corruption that results in oppression is the underlying cause of such an evil spirit, then we do have a solution—the gospel. My entire premise is that we need to be a people that live generously, with faith in Christ and His unshakeable Kingdom, rather than to allow the waves of this rising tide to bury us.

It is easy for someone living under the influence of mammon to discount what the Bible clearly states. The love of money (or the worship of mammon) is the root cause of all sorts of evil. If you read this chapter and at the end are offended and believe that I am obviously on the wrong side, you may be under the influence of something other than the Scripture or its Author. If you think that I am being too liberal in my analysis, or too conservative, the next chapter is for you.

CHAPTER FOUR

All the Demons are on the Other Side: The Rising Polarization of Worldviews

In a time of deceit, telling the truth is a revolutionary act.
—George Orwell

Only two things are infinite: the universe and human stupidity,
and I'm not sure about the former.
—Albert Einstein

TWO SPORTS RADIO TALK SHOW HOSTS were bouncing around random subjects as I inched my way forward on a jam-packed Los Angeles freeway. They concluded that almost all journalists in sports are of a liberal political point of view. The primary host openly admitted that he was indeed a liberal Democrat, and he and his guest host took some time to try to think of anyone they knew of in the industry that might hold a conservative viewpoint.

It took some time. They were struggling to come up with a single one. They freely admitted that it shouldn't be that way. The regular host said that democracy is all about a free exchange of ideas and announced that there needs to be a plurality of voices and viewpoints that are exchanged with equal opportunity and respect. Finally, the guest host mentioned one sports journalist and former athlete who is indeed conservative. The regular host responded, "Yeah, but he's a bat-crazy lunatic, so that doesn't count."

I guess ideas need to coincide with one's own point of view or they don't count. Everyone on the other side is a crazy lunatic. Such is the state of our "union." There is no listening to the other side. There is no real conversation, only belittling of each other's character. There can be no good point coming from the other side, just as there can be no sin within our own camp. We have made enemies of one another, and both sides on any debate are equally guilty.

Politically, the Right and the Left are growing farther apart with each passing week. Liberal politicians and conservatives alike are in a moral and political "take no prisoners" civil war. Each is strengthening its stance and lobbing bold and often baseless accusations at the other side. This war has spilled over into all of life, not just politics, and includes the arts, education, business, journalism, science, technology, social services, military, and the faith community.

In 2016, most people in the US were struck with a single glaring question: how did we get to a place where our only two choices for presidential candidates were so substandard? With over three hundred million people in this country, how could there not be at least one better candidate? I will attempt an explanation, but it doesn't paint a bright future for us. But first, let's take a look at the polarization itself before we examine some of the causes.

The rising polarization

A number of academic studies find evidence that polarization is on the rise. Abramowitz and Saunders conclude, "Since the 1970s, ideological polarization has increased dramatically among the mass public in the United States."[1] Based on surveys and exit poll data they conclude:

> There are now large differences in outlook between Democrats and Republicans, between red state voters and blue state voters, and between religious voters and secular voters. These divisions are not confined to a small minority of activists—they involve a large segment of the public and the deepest divisions are found among the most interested, informed, and active citizens.[2]

The Pew Research Center has tracked respondents on a ten-point ideological scale from 1994 to today. The divide between ideological viewpoints has more than doubled since 2004.[3] Among those who consider themselves politically engaged (meaning that they keep watch of political news and vote with regularity), the split is even more dramatic, as the figure below demonstrates.[4]

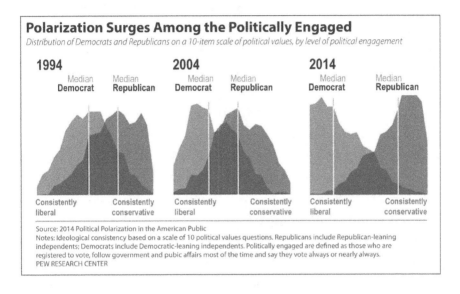

Figure 4.1

We are being torn apart, right down the middle. The only thing more alarming than this difference of opinions is the hostility with which those differences are communicated. In a recent Pew Research Center Survey, 27 percent of Democrats and 36 percent of Republicans said the opposite party's policies "are so misguided that they threaten the nation's well-being."[5] The character of anyone on the other side of the aisle is slandered not only without shame but often with self-righteous indignation.

And perhaps even more alarming is the lack of any real two-way communication over issues. There is little room for an exchange of ideas that is calm and rational, with both sides being willing to listen. In fact, the other side is labeled with the worst possible descriptions—racist, bigoted, Nazi, greedy, baby-killers, commies, or hypocrites. It is amazing how unforgiving people are of those who are on the other side, but even more incredible how easily the people on their own side are forgiven of the same or worse crimes. It can only be concluded that the greatest sin of all is simply having a different opinion.

The media is intentionally adding fuel to the conflict. Ratings rise when the on-screen debate is heated. The scenario is so predictable that watching the news on any channel has become painful. Whenever there is a lead story, we can assume that there will be two pundits representing opposing sides who have talking points from which they will not veer. They never listen to the other side except to find a foothold for their next talking point. We are not presented with fair-minded and calm experts who will delve into the issue with any depth. In fact, it is quite the opposite. Those with the most extreme viewpoints tend to be dramatic and more entertaining to watch and thus get more exposure. We are only fed extremely disparate viewpoints with no middle ground.

After some dramatic appearances on major TV news outlets, these outspoken pundits develop a following and hire ghostwriters who pen as many bestselling books as possible. Maintaining this persona is necessary to sell books and appearances, so all this blustering is continued—in fact, it is increased. People with moderate viewpoints are boring and not entertaining enough to compete with other news outlets and won't get follow-up online views and "likes" from the public, so they do not get any airtime. That is how we end up with such foolish and bombastic leaders of both sides. But it doesn't end there—it only gets started.

The fans of these pundits, emboldened by their heroes, spread the message online. The result is a more divided nation. Facebook feeds are filled with clips of their favorite pundit, blustering about various issues. Those same clips are tweeted and retweeted. All these hits encourage the news agency to continue this same endless cycle.

We can certainly argue that free speech is the heart of a democracy and a good thing. But with the power of televised media and social media, these idealistic evangelists of political persuasions have more powerful leverage over society today. Those at both the left and right ends of the spectrum, who together comprise only 20 percent of the public overall, have a greater voice on the political debates. The squeaky wheel pundits get the oil of media attention. Government representatives see these loud voices as representative of their constituency because they have so many followers (and often flatter the politician with their fanfare and fund raising). Elections are won with their sway. As a result, those elected are more extreme, and the House and Senate become more divided than ever. A few outspoken extremists end up determining our candidates. That is how we end up with such bad choices. All this will not likely change in the future…and it may get worse.

The populace is less prepared to think and reason for themselves but rely more and more on "experts" who share their worldview. One major factor in this is how we take in information via the Internet.

The Internet is dividing us

There have been other times of extreme polarization in our past. We had a bloody civil war over differences. What is different this time is that the splits are not geographical—North versus South—but extend over urban and rural, corporations and unions, people of color and law enforcement, wealthy and working class. The splits now are not over one glaring issue but have caused divisions on every possible issue.

Perhaps the greatest catalyst in polarization this time around, which accelerates the pace of the division, is the Internet. The Internet provides a voice to all people, and the louder and more obnoxious certain people are, the more exposure they get. It allows for people with wicked intentions to launch smear campaigns without any fear of repercussion. Being right and checking the facts matter little if the sound bites get hits. All the fact-checking tends to be in refutation of opposing views and is never applied with the same diligence to one's own bias.

There are four ways that the Internet has increased the pace of polarization in this country. Some of these effects are certainly being spread by other forms of media, but the Internet has put them in the palm of each person's hand virtually all day, every day.

1. Fake news: flooding the populace with lies and half-truths

I mentioned in chapter two that our language is evolving much quicker because of technology. "Fake news" is a good example of this. In a single year, this expression was born and became a principal term in "real" news stories. Of course there is nothing new about "fake news." But now we carry "fake news" sources around in our pockets all day, and these false reports are accessible instantly and passed on immediately with little to no discernment, scrutiny, or due diligence in checking the accuracy.

Armed with the anonymity of the Internet—and with no accountability—people with political agendas can devise a story that has no basis in reality. Worse yet, they can invent one that sounds like it could be true, write it up as fact, assign false documentation, and post it as a news release—and instantly and permanently damage a person's credibility.

Unfortunately, "fake news" is an easy label to attach to any news source that disagrees with us. Most people are content to simply find a source that aligns with their preset worldview and discount all other news sources. They do not want to listen to, or tolerate, a news source that challenges the opinions they already hold. The outcome? People will simply perpetuate an obstinate bias—and a deepening dislike of people who see things differently.

If we want to believe lies simply because they reinforce what we already think and make us feel better about ourselves, then we deserve to be deceived. It takes courage to question our own assumptions. It is exhausting to dig down through the shrapnel of false reports to get close to the truth. Most people decide that there are only two polar opposite points of view and feel it is in their best interest to choose one and fight the other. This is lazy, foolish, and, unfortunately, all too common.

I suggest that you never fully accept any report as complete. Hold all news sources in a place of suspicion, unworthy of your complete faith. Do this especially when they favor your own opinion. At the same time, listen for the truth that can be discovered coming from the other point of view. If you trust only one news source, you trust too many. Paraphrasing the humorist Mark Twain: "Those who do not read the news are uninformed, those who read the news are misinformed." Don't be content to stop with either.

While none of us want to be exposed as wrong, there are worse things. Isn't it better to discover you are wrong about something than to remain deluded—and wrong? These days, it is not enough that we just learn new things, but that we unlearn and relearn as well, and that is a lost but needed art in today's world.

2. Fearmongering: scaring people into high ratings and harsh opinions

Polarization requires a pull in opposite directions, and we have such a pull, constantly tugging us toward one side or the other of any issue. Fear is a primary motivator behind news outlets, real or fake. Fearmongering is when someone deliberately arouses public fear or alarm to gain a desired result.

A majority of people desire safety and security, but they live with a constant suspicion that such things are fragile and fleeting. Consequently, most people are vulnerable to manipulation by fearmongering.

Every day we get "up-to-the-minute" "Breaking News" delivered in the "Situation Room" by a man named Wolf Blitzer. You can't get scarier than that…before a single syllable of news is spoken. Fear sells the news.

Our brains are incredible information processing machines. They have to continually sort through all the stimulation and sift out the mundane from the "must-run" information they receive. Because survival is paramount to the human condition, all the information that comes through our senses must first pass through the amygdala, an almond-shaped sliver of the brain in the temporal lobe that is responsible for primal emotions such as rage, hate and fear. This provides the body with its first early warning alert, and it is always on and active, searching for any kind of threat. It is designed to enact instant response to a sudden life-threatening situation when we may not have time to think through the dangers around us. It turns on easily but takes considerably longer to shut down.

This part of the brain injects us with adrenaline so that our eyes widen, our skin becomes more sensitive, our hearing grows more acute, and our heart rate increases to make sure we have adequate oxygenated blood in all our muscles for the fight or flight that is necessary when a threat is upon us. This is how you want to be when your life is in jeopardy. But to constantly remain at this high alert can be deadly.

The news industry focuses on this part of our brain because it gets our attention the quickest and won't easily let go of our minds. Bad news sells better than good news because the amygdala is constantly looking for bad news. The saying in the journalism industry is: "If it bleeds, it leads." In these days, where our concentration is fleeting, what captures our attention first and best is the stimulation of the amygdala. Fear does this fastest and best.[6]

The response of this part of the brain is wired to continue on full alert and not to settle down until the perceived threat is eliminated. In today's world, that threat is not a leopard in a tree or a snake in the grass: it's news about a potential crisis. These potential crises hang around and never seem to leave; instead, they are constantly being pushed before us on every electronic device with an LCD screen.

In his book *False Alarm: The Truth About the Epidemic of Fear*, Dr. Marc Siegel says:

> *Statistically, the industrialized world has never been safer. Many of us are living longer and more uneventfully. Nevertheless, we live in worst-case fear scenarios. Over the past century, we Americans have dramatically reduced our risk in virtually every area of life, resulting in life spans 60 percent longer in 2000 than in 1900. Antibiotics have reduced the likelihood of dying*

from infections [...] Public health measures dictate standards for drinkable water and breathable air. Our garbage is removed quickly. We live in temperature-controlled, disease-controlled lives. And yet, we worry more than ever before. The natural dangers are no longer there, but the response mechanisms are still in place, and now they are turned on much of the time.[7]

The odds that we will be killed by a shark attack are one in 3,744,730. We often compare threats that will never truly affect us with the chances of being struck by lightning. We are three times more likely to be struck by lightning than attacked by a shark. But every time we swim out into the ocean, a shark attack from beneath is a constant nagging thought—but a bolt of lightning from above never comes into our mind. Right? This is because fear is not rational; such is the response of the amygdala. It doesn't care about the odds. It is not the rational part of your brain where statistical data bears weight. Fear is not meant to be rational; it is meant to be heeded—with urgency. And if a shark were to attack, we would be grateful for the amygdala and not care about mathematical odds, as we swam faster than we have ever swum before.

The news media is constantly stimulating the amygdala, and consequently, our brains are on constant alert. The result is that we are always paying attention but never really reflecting on what we are hearing and seeing. We end up on high alert with little rational response, only a fight or flight reaction. The other emotions that the amygdala stimulates are rage and hatred, which are also responses lacking reflection. Polarization increases because we are constantly having this part of our brains stimulated—in full color, high-def video images combined with dramatic commentary by a Blitzing Wolf from the situation room.

Both sides push their agendas this way. We are presented with potential threats that have a near zero percentage of possibility, but this part of our brain doesn't measure such things. The odds of an abortion clinic being bombed by "pro-life" supporters are practically zero, but that possibility will be brought up far more often in debate than the reality merits. Why is that? Because it draws a desired reaction in people and reinforces a narrative. The odds of being killed by terrorists who came across our borders as refugees are almost nil. Nevertheless, that scenario is often talked about as a possibility for the very same reason.

Both sides of every debate use the same tactics and yet denounce the other for "fearmongering." Some cast fear over the insecurity of our borders, a loss of jobs, the suspicion of immigrants and refugees that may be terrorists in disguise, a growing government that wants to rule over all of our lives, or the collapse of our fragile economy.

The other side warns of melting polar ice caps, an industrial war machine that makes profit off of the lost lives of our youth, racist cops hunting people of color, and Wall Street tycoons that are stealing our pensions, our homes, and polluting our water all at the same time. "Back-alley butchers" and abortion center bombers are near at hand if we do not remain vigilant against the pro-lifers.

If people on the Right have their way, we will usher in another Nazi Holocaust. If folks on the Left have their way, we will have a communist oppressor who will take our money, our land, our pension, our first born, and worst of all, our guns.

As you read the above, most of you identified some of the fears listed as legitimate and the others as mere propaganda scare tactics. I imagine that the ones you view as true threats all line up on one side of the proverbial political aisle, and the ones deemed false are on the other side. If so, you are likely under the spell of fearmongering and under the influence of political delusion. This only demonstrates that we are all afflicted with this polarization, and it alters the lenses by which we take in information. Perhaps your amygdala has more influence over your brain than you realize.

What makes these narratives sell the news so well is that they have a kernel of truth within. Any true story that reinforces the narrative of these threats gets airtime and fuels the fearmongering all the more, and is used as a way of proving a political point. Our Facebook and Twitter feeds bring us scary news stories every day. The Internet has made us all conveyors of the fear. We no longer need a Blitzing Wolf to scare us; we have all become potential broadcasters of breaking bad news.

3. The "echo chamber": cementing an opinion with constant reinforcement

In his influential book *Republic.com*, Harvard professor Cass Sunstein argues that the Internet is creating "echo chambers" where partisans hear their own opinions, biases, and prejudices endlessly reinforced. He writes: "Our communications market is rapidly moving [toward a situation where] people restrict themselves to their own points of view—liberals watching and reading mostly or only liberals; moderates, moderates; conservatives, conservatives; Neo-Nazis, Neo-Nazis."[8] This increases polarization and limits the "unplanned, unanticipated encounters [that are] central to democracy itself."[9]

Any look at the content on the Internet reveals political sites on both sides that are far more extreme than anything that existed in traditional media—and these sites have significant numbers of readers. Examining Internet comment threads or message boards reveals a level of vitriol and unabashed partisanship never seen in an old-fashioned letter to the editor or op-ed piece. The anonymity and free access of the Internet draws out the worst in humanity and puts it on display for the world to see, "like," and retweet.

According to a Pew Research Center study, Republicans on Facebook are more likely than those in other ideological groups to hear political opinions that are in line with their own views. They are also more likely to have friends who share their own political views. Two-thirds (66 percent) say most of their close friends share their views on government and politics. Democrats, on the other hand, are more likely than those in other ideological groups to block or "de-friend" someone on a social network—as well as to end a personal friendship—because of politics. They are also more likely to follow issue-based groups, rather than political parties or candidates, in their Facebook feeds.[10]

We isolate and insulate our life experience to form these pockets that feel right (or left), and thus find ourselves in our own echo chamber. We leave the chamber only long enough to make snarky comments on someone else's feed but never long enough to be influenced by another point of view.

Echo chambers, however, are not just the product of our own choices: we are being steered into them. Eli Pariser argues that Google's personalized search results and Facebook's personalized news feeds screen out content we are most likely to disagree with and create a comfortable bubble of like-minded information.[11] This is all done in an attempt to show us content we will click on, thus raising the advertising revenue. As a result we find ourselves in the echo chamber oftentimes by no choice of our own. This can have the added affect of deluding us into believing that most people share our point of view, which reinforces the polarization even more. Soon we discover that all the people we know and respect think the same as we do. "Only idiots could believe something other than what we all believe," becomes the natural thought. "The people on the opposite side must either be quacks or have some nefarious agenda because everyone who is rational agrees with me." This is the way an echo chamber solidifies a polarized worldview.[12]

Here are a few statements that can help us to see whether or not we have been duped:

If we receive all our news from only one outlet yet feel well-informed, we are deluded.

If we put stock in a report with little to no substantive evidence simply because it reinforces a similar point of view as our own, we are likely deceived.

If we think that the worst and most extreme story about the other side reveals the true character of those on that side, we are deluded.

If we easily forgive the failings of politicians from our side but never forgive politicians from the other side, we are biased.

If we think people who hold the view opposite of our own are extreme lunatics with minimal intelligence, we are deluded.

If we view every bad report about the candidate from our side as a slanderous lie from the right or left-wing conspiracy, but every good report about the candidate from the other side as mere propaganda, we are deceived.

If all our beliefs coincide with the stated policies of our party, and we can find nothing good in the values on the other side, we are deluded—and bigoted, regardless of party.

If we do not have respected friends who fall on the other side of the aisle of political beliefs, and with whom we can have a decent conversation, we are probably deluded.

If we believe that the people on our side have our best interests in mind but the other side has a selfish agenda, we are dangerously deluded.

If we think that all Democrats are communist baby-killers or all Republicans are greedy, closet racists, we are deluded.

If we believe that a totalitarian regime is only a viable threat from the other side, we are deluded.

4. Radicalization: Making each of us a shallow evangelist of a worldview

While these first three issues are all part of the problem we face, I contend that the effects of the Internet are far more insidious. The way we digest information on the Internet may actually be radicalizing people faster than Isis or Al-Qaeda combined.

Not only does the Internet misinform us and instill fear in us with constant reinforcement, it may also cause us to be morally and mentally shallow. This is how radicalization occurs, and it is not something solely reserved for religious fanatics.

Many Christians hear the word "radicalization" and wonder why we wouldn't want such an objective. We want radical faith that is willing to go anywhere and do whatever God asks of us, no doubt. But radicalization—a growing study within the fields of sociology, psychology and neuroscience—is not something we should desire.

Radicalization is when a person is indoctrinated without deep reflection and void of the sobering reality of life experience among people of varying viewpoints. It makes fanatics of those who do not think for themselves and do not care about the well-being of others, but instead are driven simply by the agendas of their cause and those who instruct them. I contend that the Internet and news media are making radicals of us all.

Studies in Canada are finding a correlation between high social media consumption and a decrease of one's moral standards.[13] My colleague Jessie Cruickshank is a Harvard trained neuroscientist and an expert on how the brain works and learns. In a seminal article identifying the Internet as a 4th space (1st space is your home, 2nd space is your workplace, 3rd space is your social world),[14] she mentions a few Canadian studies proposing the shallowing of morality among those fully engaging in social media and puts forward her own analysis.[15] She writes:

> Part of the struggle with the high engagement of social media use is the lack of reflection it allows. In the mind, one can be externally focused, or internally reflective, but not both at the same time. The internally reflective state is interrelated with a person's long-term memory, social-emotions such as empathy and compassion, as well as their ability to think about the future and consequences of their actions. While there is not a "moral center" in the brain, these neurological functions are related to morality. This means that there are potentially significant consequences to consistent and persistent lack of internal reflection [such as is found among those tethered to social media].[16]

Cruickshank explains that there are two types of long-term memory systems in our brains: semantic and episodic. Semantic memory accumulates facts and concepts, which can help us win points on Jeopardy or pass a written test in school. It is easily forgotten and recycled and therefore rarely contributes to changing our lives in any meaningful way.[17]

In contrast, episodic memory consists of both procedural memory (driving a car, brushing our teeth, or shooting a free throw) and autobiographical memory (our story). Autobiographical memory is the long-term memory system interconnected with social emotions such as empathy and compassion, while semantic memory does not interact with those emotive qualities. When learning is void of hands-on experience that can lock it away into autobiographical memory, it remains a shallow type of learning within the semantic system, void of relational connectivity. We simply cannot feel empathy or compassion without any personal reference point within our autobiographical memory that can unlock those feelings.

We can be vocal and committed to what is stored in the semantic memory system, but it can be a cold and unsympathetic commitment because it is a commitment to a point of view or an idea isolated from our own human experience. This fosters a type of radicalization.

Jessie explains:

> To be clear, the worst thing one can do, in my opinion, is have decontextualized statements, tweets, posts, videos, and blogs that are overly simplistic, dehumanize, vilify, or offer final answers and applications. Learning is meant to be a journey and short-cutting the journey creates radicalized people, Internet trolls, and those who are "educated beyond their obedience."[18]

Instruction via the Internet is possible without causing radicalization, but it requires a different approach than we are accustomed to. It requires that we digest the concepts in real relationships and learn via reflection, experience, and interaction with people who are different. Each idea conveyed would need to be digested away from the LCD screen and bounced around in real life within relationships before it is considered "learned."

That, however, is not how information is received by the masses. In other words, the very way information is processed by most people is by creating followers of a point of view with high levels of commitment but shallow experience, void of relational emotions such as empathy. Our current culture is multiplying the number of volatile, outspoken, and shallow adherents of worldviews (liberal or conservative) with no love and compassion, and it is doing so at an exploding rate. This situation radicalizes people and at the same time provides them with a platform to proclaim their ideas and troll those who don't hold to the same point of view.

Dumbing us down and firing us up

Any of these four ways the Internet is affecting us is serious in and of itself. As these influences combine, polarization is elevated at an exponential rate. People are more and more deceived by incomplete disinformation (fake news) that is reinforced in an increasing echo chamber designed to incite a fearful reaction and a radicalization of people who think and act with shallow morality. Recent studies even show that when we are presented with challenging information, our ability to remember context and details decreases.[19] The very means of what is thrust upon us so quickly and urgently by news media actually dumbs us down as it elevates our fear. It could be that the "news" is actually making us less intelligent, not better informed.

The human brain is a willing accomplice to the insidious nature of how we collect information. Cruickshank explains that the brain is efficient and "inherently lazy." It is designed to sift through loads of information and remember only what reinforces its current knowledge. We don't even see things that are contrary to what we already believe, so we are, in one sense, blind to opposing thought. Ninety-nine percent of all the stimulation and potential input that comes at us is filtered out by our minds, before the media and the Internet begin to manipulate us. Jessie comments, "We don't even see things that are not in our worldview—they are literally not part of our reality." Then, what our brain does see is incorporated as evidence for our worldview—this is confirmation bias. Even if it inherently does not conform to our worldview, our brain contorts it to make it fit.

These four effects combine, causing us to get stuck in a confirmation bias loop that never reflects or sympathizes with others. We end up ignorant and more outspoken about it.

Before we start to point our fingers at one side or another, it is important that we realize that we are willing accomplices to the dumbing down and polarization of worldviews going on all around us. It's our own fault.

You are not alone—but the solution starts with you

This chapter has focused on the fourth and final rising global trend addressed in this book. There is one aspect that separates this chapter from the previous three. In the first three—rising population, rising technological advances, and the rising financial gap—we find ourselves powerless to change things and must simply raise our awareness and find a way to do our good work in the midst of the changes. With polarization, however, I believe we can make a difference, or at the very least *be* different. We can find a way to be less deluded and stop contributing to the problem.

It may be hard for any of us to read this chapter and accept that we have been duped. Misery loves company. If it helps you feel better, these factors have affected us all. Below are a few things that may make it somewhat easier to accept that we have been deceived.

1. *You are not alone.* This deception is a universal phenomenon, and all of us have been subject to it. Even the smartest and most informed people alive are mistaken about some things. The truly intelligent people are those who realize it and are courageous enough to change.

2. *You are in new territory that has never been trodden, so mistakes*

are the only way to learn. Everyone is walking on new ground here, and so we must all be the trailblazers who figure this out first. If we reach the end of the trail and find it doesn't lead to where we wanted to go, we can do one of two things: either name the new place after the desired place (i.e. call the indigenous people 'Indians' and later tell the world we discovered America), or go back and try again. That is how pioneers blaze new trails.

3.   *You are doing the best you can with the poor choices presented to you.* Like the presidential election of 2016, we may believe we are presented without any good choice and must choose what we deem the lesser of two evils. Whatever choice we made is no worse or better than the choices made by others. While not a solution, this levels the playing field a bit.

4.   *Finding the rock-bottom truth is near impossible today.* We are all drowning in false information and partial truths, so it is almost impossible to know what is real and what is just a public image. One day, what is done in secret will be proclaimed and exposed to all, but until that time we must become more comfortable not knowing all the facts and living in faith that one day we will.

5.   *Every day you can start over.* We do not have to continue living in deceit and being used. We can wake up one morning and decide that we will no longer be a mouthpiece for a biased worldview that is full of hatred and bigotry. We are not just to love those who hold the same opinions as us. We are also to love our neighbors, no matter what point of view they have. Beyond that, Jesus commands that we even love our enemies and pray for those who hate us. If this is impossible for us, then we are not living a life connected to Jesus. Many people are nominal and cultural Christians, without a true relationship with God. Such people cannot have the kind of miraculous love of others that Jesus brings.

These statements can help us see that being deluded in these days is common and can be corrected. It is not those who have been deceived that are the fools today, but rather, those who choose to remain in delusion after facing some of the facts. Don't remain a dupe of others.

Don't deflect your own responsibility by ramping up charges against the other side without any personal reflection of your own weaknesses. Remaining in delusion after being confronted with truth is worse than just being duped in the first place.

As followers of Jesus, we need to love all people: those like us, those unlike us, and those who don't like us. Such is the way of Jesus. It is the calling we have received. In fact, there is no higher calling on our lives than to love. All other agendas in this world are secondary. Being right, showing others' wrongs, and altering our culture are all meaningless distractions away from loving our neighbor as ourselves. Those who are loving will also be moral, but it is all too common to find supposedly "moral" people void of love and overflowing with judgment and spite.

Implications for our place in the world

There are consequences of the trend of increasing polarization for both local churches and the universal Church that I believe we should notice.

The white evangelical Church is now hitched to the right-wing conservative movement that put Donald Trump into office. It is widely reported that 81 percent of the white evangelical vote went for Trump. No matter what good is accomplished in the next few years, Trump's election will be postured by the media as a serious mistake, and the Church will bear the blame. The narrative will be that Trump won on the backs of the alt-right. Hateful racists and the white evangelical church will be lumped together and condemned as committing a serious mistake.

The perception that evangelicals are increasingly hypocritical appears to be rising at an incredible rate—and not without reason. In 2011, the Public Religion Research Institute (PRRI) asked voters if an elected official who commits immoral acts in their personal life can still behave ethically and fulfill their public and professional duties. In the study results, white evangelical Protestants were the least forgiving. Sixty-one percent said such a politician could not "behave ethically"—twice the 30 percent who felt that such a politician could manage it.

Five years later, in October 2016, PRRI asked the same question. The percentage of white evangelical Protestants who said that a politician who commits an immoral act in their personal life could still behave ethically shot up from 30 to 72 percent. The percentage saying such a politician could not serve ethically plunged from 63 to 20 percent.[20] "In a head-spinning reversal," Robert P. Jones, the C.E.O. of PRRI, wrote in the July 2017 issue of *The Atlantic*, "white evangelicals went from being the least likely to the most likely group to agree that a candidate's personal immorality has no bearing on his performance in public office."[21] Why? There can only be one reason: Donald Trump.

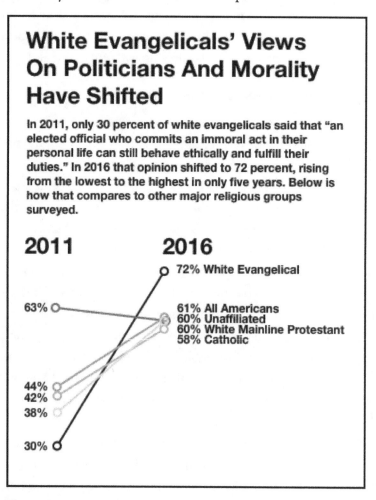

White Evangelicals' Views On Politicians And Morality Have Shifted

In 2011, only 30 percent of white evangelicals said that "an elected official who commits an immoral act in their personal life can still behave ethically and fulfill their duties." In 2016 that opinion shifted to 72 percent, rising from the lowest to the highest in only five years. Below is how that compares to other major religious groups surveyed.

2011   **2016**

72% White Evangelical

63%   61% All Americans
              60% Unaffiliated
              60% White Mainline Protestant
              58% Catholic

44%
42%
38%

30%

Figure 4.2

Bigotry, hate, and racism, combined with obvious hypocrisy, will be the leverage used to break down and destroy the organized church. It doesn't take a prophet to see that writing on the wall. As followers of Jesus Christ, we will experience legal, moral, and spiritual assault in the days that are to come. We must ready ourselves.

I believe we can only find strength in this: unconditional love for all people. The more we stand up against this rising trend with political reaction, desperate to cling to something that we will never be allowed to keep, the more we actually help those who seek to destroy us. In that way, we have become the instrument of our own undoing. That war has already been lost. Politics was never a hope worthy of our faith. It now has become an idol that steals it.

The civil war is hot, and neither side is at all close to building bridges or bringing peace. We simply must take a different approach if we want to make a difference in this world—and now is the time. But in order to *make* a difference, we must first *be* different.

Today's emerging generation is fed up with an unengaged, judgmental Christianity that is afraid to get its hands dirty with real change but is more than willing to tell everyone else how bad they are.

The same old thing never changed anything. There is only one thing that can truly change this world, and His name is Jesus.

PART TWO

Surviving the Soon:
Perched on the Precipice

CHAPTER FIVE

We Can No Longer Afford to Stay Where We Are

A time will come when instead of shepherds feeding the sheep,
the Church will have clowns entertaining the goats.
—Charles Haddon Spurgeon

When we least expect it, life sets us a challenge to test our courage and
willingness to change; at such a moment, there is no point in pretending that
nothing has happened or in saying that we are not yet ready. The challenge
will not wait. Life does not look back. A week is more than enough time
for us to decide whether or not to accept our destiny.
—Paulo Coelho

ANY ONE OF THE RISING TRENDS MENTIONED in the previous section should be enough to awaken us to a new way of relating to God, one another, and the chaotic world we swim in. Taken together, however, they raise the stakes to a level where we simply must wake up now. Time is crucial with the increasing scale and velocity of change. Every moment wasted is a doubling of the challenge we face.

The church model as we have experienced it over the centuries is incapable of meeting the challenges of this age. If it were a solution, we would have found our traction by now. We haven't. We continue to celebrate the success of ever-larger churches that grow by addition of new members from dying smaller churches as if we are making a difference in this world. All the while we are sliding further away from any significance at all.

The institutional model of church first established by the Constantine regime didn't fulfill the Great Commission in its own time with only a fraction of the population we are now called to reach. In fact, it is quite clear that the more organic expression of church prior to Emperor Constantine's rise to power (and the subsequent elevation of Christendom to a government endorsed institution) did far better at reaching the nations than its more public and politically powerful later model.

If the "Sunday morning song, sermon, and say a prayer" model didn't work when the population was only a few hundred million, why would we keep trying to make it work now when the population is fast approaching eight billion? In this chapter I will demonstrate three reasons why we can no longer continue to bet on a very old horse that never won a race in its youth.

1. Our current church model is incapable of multiplying

I see a big difference between the *attractional* model of church and the *missional* model. An attractional model will not reproduce and multiply—it can only add. Growth by addition is just not enough to keep up because the population of the world is so rapidly multiplying. Adding services or video venue sites is not multiplying. Stop calling it that. Multiplication occurs when the offspring birth offspring that birth offspring. Without multiple generations, there is no multiplication, only addition. Don't say we are multiplying until we get to the fourth generation (2 Timothy 2:2).

The more expensive the church building is and the more there is a demand for professional leadership to conduct the ministry, the less likely there will be any multiplication. This has been proven time and again.

Addition is not bad—it is better than subtraction or division—but it is not the multiplication needed to reach this world. If we are so engulfed in addition methodology that we cannot change, we will forfeit our call on this planet. The first commandment God gave to man was to multiply. The last command Jesus gave His disciples carried with it the idea of multiplying.[1] This is not an option: it is our mandate.

2. The cost is too high

The typical attractional church model costs too much to multiply effectively. Salaries, rents/mortgages, equipment, advertising—the list of expenses is long. Even in the US, where churches are given tax breaks, they are struggling to make ends meet. Many people in church work are feeling the resources drying up. Recently I was in a pastors' meeting where many were wondering how their churches would continue. Some were selling their facilities just for survival.

Survival is one thing, but reaching a city is quite another. When it comes to missional effectiveness, the attractional model is just too expensive. I have seen a report conducted by a large denomination to determine what it would cost to reach the US. They had the courage to ask the question and punch the calculator—but not to publish the results publicly, so it remains mostly hidden.

In the report, the financial costs to reach particular cities for Christ using the traditional attractional model of church are listed. The results are alarming. To reach one city alone would be astronomical. The study shows that to reach Atlanta would cost over $63 billion. To reach New York City would cost much more: $418 billion.

Giving USA, a non-profit foundation that studies philanthropy in the United States, found a total of $119.3 billion went to houses of worship and denominational organizations in 2015. But that is down about 50 percent since 1990, and the percentage has been "in steady decline for some time."[2] If we plug that number into the formula used in the previous paragraph, that entire amount could only reach the greater Washington DC area and would leave the rest of our country lost. But of course, if it did go to that cause, it would not cover any of the costs of all our current churches and ministries, and they would all go out of business. This says nothing of reaching the rest of the world.

Clearly the attractional model is not a viable solution to reach our world. We could reach the cities faster and for a fraction of the cost with a simpler approach to church. I believe that we must lower the bar of how we do church and raise the bar of what it means to be a disciple if we want to reach this world with the good news.

We need to be about the reproduction of healthy disciples, leaders, churches, and movements—in that order. I am not suggesting we shut down churches or sell off all our property. I am suggesting we invest more energy and attention in simpler opportunities all around us. We cannot focus on trying to reproduce complex and expensive systems if we do not first reproduce the simple and more basic entities. If reproducing disciples is too much to ask, then certainly reproducing churches full of them is impossible, right? Don't start churches to make disciples. Make disciples—and churches will start far more easily.

3. The attractional model—isn't

A current phrase to describe the old church paradigm is "attractional model." That term, coined by Alan Hirsch and Mike Frost,[3] describes the idea behind why a church works so hard to get better at doing what it has always been doing. The perception is that if a church puts on a production that will amaze, amuse, and amass people, it will ultimately draw them to Jesus.

This good motive, invested poorly, takes us to some rather peculiar places. "Church" has become an event that we attend and experience rather than a family we are part of. As such, it looks more like a show designed to please people. The larger attractional churches have more resources and end up with better shows and consequently, more people. Churches compete with one another to attract more people to the show.

In the end, church is evaluated as either a success or a failure based on its appeal to people—which should be the very last criteria. This is especially true when someone chooses to leave one church for another. It is not rare to hear remarks like these:

"I wasn't getting fed there;"

"The children's ministry over here is so much better than the other church— we couldn't help but switch churches;"

"I didn't like the music at my old church."

Our language betrays misguided motives. When our success is

determined by something we call "attendance," then we are actually producing an event, not developing a family or deploying a movement. You don't attend a family or a movement. You attend a show.

In fact, if our aim is to launch a movement, then "attendance" is the opposite of the goal, right? Think about that. By very definition, a movement is mobile, not static or stationary. It doesn't have an address. You can spread a movement, bear the message of a movement, be part of a movement, even launch a movement—but you cannot attend one.

To be fair, much of our practice as churches is inherited from centuries of thought, passed along to us. Most Christians simply assume these traditions are what God wants and what the Bible teaches. Many church leaders spend sleepless nights thinking about how to improve their event to draw more people in to attend. They are praying for souls to be saved, bodies to be baptized, and members to be numbered. But in truth, all our practices expose us wanting to lure Christians from other churches to our own.

The world is no longer wanting to get up early on Sunday morning, dress up on a day off, and go to a church service where they sing love songs to a man they've never met, give money, and hear a lecture. Does this sound like a viable strategy to reach people for Christ? Is it even a sound means to attract people to church? Would you spend billions of dollars to accomplish this strategy, believing it will change the world? Sadly, Christians have done so for far too long. In fact, that is the dominant strategy of the evangelical Western Church in this century, and it is yielding the results you would expect.

Only Christians would be attracted to this sort of event. I cannot think of a single non-Christian that would say they want some of that. We, the initiated, understand the culture of Sunday worship services and are comfortable with the proceedings.

Those who come to a service with us but who are not in our cultural tribe don't understand how we can sing a love song as Jesus' beloved bride and two minutes later sing about being His child. What?! Mixing metaphors is always a bad idea, but I can't think of a more horrendous mistake than this one. The uninitiated hear something like that, and it raises all kinds of red flags, and rightfully so. Frankly, I don't get it. Do you? Is there a coherent theology behind our worship practices?

Church worship bands rehearse for worship services. This idea raises some questions that perhaps we have not thought to ask. How do you rehearse worship? Is it something you practice over and over again to get right so that when you actually do it for God on Sunday morning it is better than if you just did it the first time? If indeed the idea is to improve our worship so that God likes it better, shouldn't the entire congregation be practicing? Can you actually get so good that even God is impressed by your craft? Of course not. Let's be honest. We are not rehearsing worship to improve for God's acceptance, but for those we are actually trying to reach—attenders.

Christians, whether true believers or just those who identify with Christian microculture, form the only population segment in our culture that is programmed to accept such an event without question. The questions raised in the above paragraphs are likely the first time most reading this book have ever thought of them.

When we work hard to make the event that takes place in most church buildings on Sunday mornings better, we are actually only working harder to attract more Christians. There really isn't any other way to see this. And the audience of favorable Christians is now waking up to the fact that even they don't enjoy it anymore. Why do we continue to push this event as though God Himself commanded it? He didn't. Nowhere in the Bible is such an activity prescribed, taught, encouraged, or modeled.

Do we really think that our God is so small that we must endure a song, sermon, and prayer once a week on Sunday or He will lose His patience and smite us? Will we find blessings from God because we do these things and forfeit them if we do not? No. Jesus spent no time doing such and never instructed us to do so either. In fact, He is quite clear about the sort of activity He desires.

Jesus said,

> *"Then the King will say to those on his right, 'Come, you who*
> *are blessed by my Father; take your inheritance, the kingdom*
> *prepared for you since the creation of the world. For I was*
> *hungry and you gave me something to eat, I was thirsty and you*
> *gave me something to drink, I was a stranger and you invited*
> *me in, I needed clothes and you clothed me, I was sick and you*
> *looked after me, I was in prison and you came to visit me.'"*
> MATTHEW 25:34-36 NIV

Giving food and drink to the hungry and thirsty are what He desires. Hosting the stranger, providing clothes to the poor, visiting those in prison, and caring for the sick are on His short list of activities He wants to see. Those who do these things are welcomed to join Him and share in the inheritance of heaven. When we do such things for the poor, the stranger, the infirmed, and the prisoner, we are doing it for Jesus (that is worship). There is nothing in Jesus' words about church service attendance, sermons to the faithful, tithing, or membership. Nothing.

We've been taught that singing praise songs and giving 10 percent of our money at a service on Sunday brings pleasure to Jesus, but it is actually acts of kindness to the poor and desperately broken that bring Him pleasure.

More shocking is that those who do not love the hurting as Jesus describes will find they are not accepted, even if they participate faithfully each week in a worship service (Matthew 25:41-46).

Frankly, the type of love and service Jesus described and desires is far more attractive to us, to the world, and to God, than some contemporary praise songs and an uplifting sermon complete with jokes and an inspiring anecdote. We should be more consumed with being self-sacrificing and loving people than managing a service each week. Sadly, we have placed far more emphasis on our weekly worship service than on our daily service of those in need. This is way out of balance and just plain wrong.

So if indeed it is true that our current expressions of church are incapable of reaching the masses and cost too much to even reach a town or neighborhood, why do we continue with them? In fact, we don't just continue to let them happen, we invest in them even more, hoping to make them better, more relevant, and eventually successful.

Am I suggesting that we disband the established churches? No, I am not. There is nothing wrong with the saints gathering to worship or hear a sermon. It may not be the command of Scripture, but it can be helpful for some. Let's recognize, however, that a follower of Christ may pass up attending such an event, and it doesn't mean they are less spiritual or less obedient.

What I am suggesting is that we place a higher priority on being the type of disciple throughout the week that is out in the world making a difference in the ways that our Lord described. I suggest that we shift our investments to helping the poor and the hurting and spend less on ourselves. I suggest that we become disciples worth reproducing. Perhaps then we will see the multiplication we long to see.

Until then, our current expressions of church not only greatly reduce our value in the world, but they also increase our vulnerability. The next chapter exposes some of our obvious vulnerabilities.

CHAPTER SIX

Vulnerabilities of the Church

Never be afraid to trust an unknown future to a known God.
—Corrie Ten Boom

The illiterate of the 21st century will not be those who cannot read and write,
but those who cannot learn, unlearn, and relearn.
—Alvin Toffler

IN THE 1970s, missionaries from Mennonite churches in America started some churches in Ethiopia. When the indigenous church was self-sufficient, the Americans returned home. There were about 5,000 Ethiopian members meeting in churches, and the missionaries felt they had done a good job. They had no idea.

In 1982, communists took over that country, and the persecution of the churches was immediate and severe. All buildings were confiscated. All leaders were imprisoned, killed, or forced into exile. Church members were forbidden to meet, and evangelism was illegal. All public expression of church immediately ceased. The Mennonite church was driven underground and forced to survive without buildings, leaders, or any public service.

This persecution in Ethiopia lasted ten years. By 1992, the communist regime ended, and the Mennonites could once again come out of hiding and assemble. To everyone's shock, there were now 50,000 church members.[1]

In ten years, without the usual trappings of property, pastors, or programs, the Church multiplied tenfold. This is not an unusual story at all. In fact, historically it is normative.

I often wonder what would happen if such a challenge faced our churches? Would our people pass the test of persecution? Are we discipling in such a way that our people are persecution-proof? Sadly, I fear most churches are unprepared.

Two missing phenomena in the Western Church

I am convinced that there are two related conditions we have not experienced in the Western Church in recent days: rapid multiplication movements and persecution. These two conditions are directly related to one another, though their sources are quite opposite.

I believe that we are not persecuted, simply because our enemy is content with our current condition. Why would he try to mess up the Church when we have done so for him, with our selfish ambition, fearful insecurity, competitive spirit, and greed? Our influence is marginalized in society, and church members, rightly or wrongly, are believed to be hateful and selfish people—the opposite of Jesus. Satan is quite content with a once-a-week, consumer-driven model of church that is a mere shell of what we are supposed to be.

The second thing we haven't experienced in Western churches is rapid multiplication, and I believe that is not due to the enemy, but to God. Frankly, God doesn't want to multiply our current expressions of church because He doesn't want more of them. Unhealthy things tend to become infertile, losing the ability to reproduce. It is the natural design of creation that the fit survive and reproduce, and the weak and sick do not.

We must see these two factors change. No one wants persecution, but its absence is somewhat alarming in the scope of history. Why? Because it is promised to those who are godly (2 Timothy 3:12). The more we are like Jesus, the more we will experience persecution. That is the promise of the Scriptures (John 15:18-25). Its absence, therefore, is quite revealing and alarming.

The good news is that these phenomena will both change with only one solution: when we become a healthy and obedient church. God will want to multiply a type of church that is responsive to Him and compassionate to the world, and the enemy will mobilize his efforts to resist it. After years of traveling all over North America, Asia and Europe, I am delighted to say that we are finally on the verge of seeing these things happen.

The Church is becoming healthier and more indigenous. I am seeing ordinary people empowered to carry the work of God's Kingdom out of the meeting place and into the marketplace where it is a threat to our common enemy. I believe multiplication and persecution are not far away.

Preparing for what is to come

In 2000, we launched what is now called the organic church movement. It was a simpler and more relationally based expression of church that could multiply more easily. We doubled the number of churches in this movement every succeeding year and spread across the globe.[2]

I'm often asked if I feel that our organic church movement has accomplished all that I had hoped. The answer is no. We are not the movement that I hoped for—*yet*. But that is partly because I have always felt that what we were doing was preparing the Church for what is coming: persecution. I see our work as sowing seeds for a future harvest, and I believe that future is getting closer every day.

In all of history, the freedom to worship we have experienced in our lifetime is actually an anomaly. The Bible makes clear that those who follow Christ will be hated and will endure persecution. There is good reason to expect that persecution will arise as those who follow Christ become godlier, more on mission and fruitful. If I am wrong and persecution doesn't come, I have not lost anything. But if it does and we are unprepared, then we have lost much. I feel called to prepare God's people for a future that is less open and free but far more fruitful.

One of the heroes of my faith is Watchman Nee. God used him (and others like him) to prepare the Church in China before the communist revolution took over. He launched the "Little Flock" movement, which was a radical departure from the Western church model that had been originally planted in China. Nee's movement was smaller, simpler in structure, inexpensive, and indigenous. The churches met in smaller gatherings in homes, led by ordinary people with real jobs.

When the communists took power, they arrested the church leaders (like Nee), seized all church property, kicked out all missionaries, and burned all Christian literature. But the indigenous expressions of simple churches meeting in homes not only survived, they *thrived*. The Cultural Revolution of Mao Zedong sought to eliminate all religion from society in China, but instead it mobilized the Church, causing it to grow from about two million Christians in 1949 to over sixty million.[3] It is estimated today that there may be upward of 160 million Christians in China, representing approximately 12 percent of the entire population.[4]

Contrast this with the Church of Russia. The Russian church was dependent upon three things: holy buildings, holy men in robes, and holy services performed on holy days by those men in those robes and in those buildings. When the communists took over Russia, they seized all the buildings and arrested or compromised all the leaders of the Church. The Church of Russia was devastated. It did not thrive. Granted, there was a remnant that struggled to survive underground, but those Christ-followers were not able to see the exponential growth the Chinese church did. The Church of China prepared in advance and was ready. The Church in Russia was not ready, and it did not thrive.

Deep within, I carry a feeling that everything I have been about for the past thirty years is just preparing the Bride of Christ for what is to come. In fact, *CMA (Church Multiplication Associates)*, the *organic church movement, 100Movements* and *Starling Initiatives* were all birthed to prepare God's Church for what is to come. Like Nee, these endeavors have been striving to bring health and simplicity back to the Church and an ability to ride out any storm that will come. This book is written in that same spirit.

The vulnerability of the Church in the West

Imagine you are in an episode of Star Trek where you wind up on some strange planet, complete with fake boulders and painted murals of two moons behind you. You are captured for the entertainment of the gods who inhabit the planet, and you have to fight like a gladiator against a wild beast. You must choose between two weapons: a machine gun or a bazooka. You can also choose your foe: an angry, mutant bear twice the normal size, or an ordinary swarm of agitated killer bees. What choices do you make?

Even though the fierce bear may be terrifying in appearance, and a single bee may seem small and insignificant (sans allergies), a swarm of bees is something you cannot stop with such weapons. Either weapon would help against the bear, but there is no weapon that can truly stop a swarm of bees.

The Church in the West is a large, clumsy beast, easily taken down with any choice of weapon. What we need is to become more swarm-like in our expression. Only then can we thrive and multiply against the attacks that are coming.

I do not think persecution is so far off. What would it take for it to become reality? Not much. I believe the pieces are already on the board and being pushed into play. Truthfully, however, I think most churches are so anemic that they could be shut down before any real persecution ever occurs. Does that sound overly pessimistic?

The large churches in the West are far more vulnerable than most care to admit. With the rapid rise of the megachurch, the Church in general has become more centralized, more expensive, and more personality driven and consumer oriented. In fact, as many smaller churches close and their people assimilate into the larger ones, we have actually concentrated all our people, resources, and ideas into a few large targets rather than many smaller autonomous ones. We have moved in the opposite direction from a swarm mentality. We have also seen that these larger churches are more dependent upon single charismatic leaders. Take these leaders out or compromise them, and the whole church suffers greatly. We are regularly seeing some of these large "successful" churches struggle after the departure of their dynamic leader.

Let me map out a few steps that would permanently alter church as we have known it. It actually wouldn't take persecution to close many churches down, just a few legal changes that are already being considered.

Churches in the US are granted very generous tax privileges. There are three that allow for a great number of churches to survive with less income. Churches have less to pay for land, offer incentive for people giving to write off on their taxes and the money received for personnel can spread farther. If the following benefits were revoked, many churches would be forced to close: the tax deduction for contributions, property tax exemptions, and the parsonage allowance. I say this because the way we do church is so expensive that we rely upon these special privileges to survive. This is especially true in a struggling economy where our government is looking for ways to reduce its deficit and increase tax revenue to provide more services for its constituents—services, by the way, that most churches no longer supply to their communities.

If you are a leader of a church, as you read this I suggest that you ask yourself how your church would survive if these three tax benefits were revoked. That is far better than to simply write off what I am saying by telling yourself this could never happen. Crunch the numbers. Do the math. It will be scary but may lead you to take some sound steps to be better prepared.

1. Removing the parsonage allowance

Few ordinary citizens know about this special perk that pastors get. I have enjoyed this benefit, and honestly I don't even know why it is available to me. All money spent on housing (rent/mortgage, utilities, furniture, home improvements/repairs/upkeep/supplies) can be written off the salary of a paid church leader even up to the entire amount they are paid in salary. I actually feel like I am betraying our "special club" for even speaking of it publicly. Add the fact that church leaders are able to opt out of Social Security, and you can easily see how pastors are able to get by on a much lower actual salary than most people. If you don't think churches rely upon this, your head is in the sand.

A pastoral staff can literally double with this benefit, allowing a church to maintain a professional staff twice the size that it can actually afford. There are not many churches in the West that feel like they have more staff than they need. Most churches have far more ministry than they have leaders. The more a church relies upon professional staff, the more vulnerable it is to the potential loss of this perk.

I cannot imagine what sort of argument churches could possibly raise to defend this benefit in the eyes of the populace. Whatever is said will just sound like the whining of a privileged toddler, crying because it will be treated like everyone else. Pastors, we should all be prepared to lose this perk.

2. Removing the property tax exemption

What would happen if our churches were forced to pay taxes on their property? This would push most churches over the edge of viability, at least in their current form—especially if the other perks mentioned were also removed.

Most cities are already openly hostile to churches and try to prevent them from acquiring property because there is no tax income from these organizations. I can only imagine that the city of Houston is glaring at Lakewood Church's $32 million per year income and wondering what the property taxes should be. Before Lakewood Church bought the building outright, the Houston Rockets basketball team used the same space more often during the week, provided far better entertainment value (including two NBA championships), and paid their fair share of taxes to support the infrastructure of the community.

Most city officials see the local Denny's Restaurant as more beneficial to their community than the local church. Ouch. Why? Because the restaurant provides meals, a public gathering place, jobs, and taxes. The local church usually provides none of those things. No wonder there is increasingly unapologetic hostility toward churches looking to purchase property in neighborhoods across the US.

3. Removing tax deductions for contributions

If people could no longer write off their financial contributions to churches, I am sure that many churches would see their annual income drop severely. We would like to think it isn't so, but why else is it that churches count on larger gifts at the end of the year? It's because people are looking for a tax benefit. Granted, this is likely the last perk to be removed because so many other non-profit organizations also benefit from this.

Nevertheless, this is also a vulnerability of the Church as we know it. We would like to think that our people are generous merely out of love and respect for Jesus and His Kingdom. I'm sure that some are. But I am equally sure that many donate simply because it benefits their tax status and they would rather control where their money goes than just fork it over to the government.

How will the Church respond?

In the US, Christians already have a reputation of being intolerant. Evangelical and fundamental expressions of Christianity that are too closely tied to the Tea Party and Republican agendas have consistently decried those who have what are called "special entitlements." This will set us up for public mockery—something we should be used to by now. When these laws take our own "entitlements" away and we are found complaining louder than the rest, our reputation as hypocrites will be confirmed in the eyes of the world and will only expedite passage of these measures. These laws can easily be viewed by the public as a way that the Church is subsidized by the government, because, indeed they are. A true separation of church and state would cut these off.

It's a simple scenario that is very possible. Is your church getting ready?

Like the Russian church prior to communism, our churches are dependent upon holy buildings (remove property tax exemption) and holy men or women (remove parsonage allowance) that perform holy practices in those buildings (remove tax deductible donations). Our vulnerability is quite obvious. These three areas of dependence could take us out. We must decrease our dependence upon buildings, budgets, and big shots. We must also respond to our society with love rather than with lobbying for self-interested legislature to protect our privileges.

Church leaders need to be considering these possibilities and taking steps to be prepared. I firmly believe that the more we move toward an incarnational, missional and movemental expression of church, the better prepared we will be. We must adopt more of a swarm mentality to survive and thrive in the coming days. Then no weapon fashioned against us will be able to stop us.

PART THREE

Delivering on our Destiny: Finding a Future-Proof Faith

CHAPTER SEVEN

Being Different in this Different World: Excel in the Now

With the past, I have nothing to do; nor with the future. I live now.
—Ralph Waldo Emerson

We cannot always build the future for our youth,
but we can build our youth for the future.
—Franklin D. Roosevelt

IT IS A STRANGE THING that so many church organizations want to change the world by becoming relevant to it. But in order to be relevant to the world, they strive to become more like it—and it ends up changing them. A strange irony indeed.

My friend Keith Giles has said, "We can't transform a culture if that culture has already transformed us."[1]

Given the rapid changes occurring in our world right now, a question posed by the late philosopher Francis Schaeffer is more significant than ever: *how should we then live?*[2] How do these dramatic shifts affecting the world (population growth, technological advancements, economic redistribution, and rising polarization) affect the Church and those who would follow Christ?

In order to thrive in these rapidly changing days, we must make some adjustments. Every day that we delay in making changes, we become rapidly less influential and increasingly insignificant. Our irrelevance is already spiking on the exponential growth curve as is. Each week that we neglect to change, we fall back by miles, not inches. To survive we must embrace a different mindset, and we must do it immediately.

One of the mottoes at Google's X research and development lab is "Fail fast." Eric Teller tells his teams: "I don't care how much progress you make this month; my job is to cause your rate of improvement to increase—how do we make the same mistake in half the time for half the money?"[3]

Thomas Friedman summarizes Teller's philosophy of adaptation:

> What we are experiencing today, with shorter and shorter innovation cycles, and less and less time to learn to adapt, "is the difference between a constant state of destabilization versus occasional destabilization." The time of static stability has passed us by, he [Teller] added. That does not mean we can't have a new kind of stability, "but the new kind of stability has to be dynamic stability. There are some ways of being, like riding a bicycle, where you cannot stand still, but once you are moving it is actually easier. It is not our natural state. But humanity has to learn to exist in this state." We're all going to have to learn that bicycle trick. When that happens, said Teller, "in a weird way we will be calm again, but it will take substantial relearning. We definitely don't train our children for dynamic stability."[4]

It is obvious that among all the social institutions of life, the local church has been the least able to adapt to change. Trying to hold on to stability in a world that is changing so rapidly is as foolish as rearranging the furniture on the Titanic. The good news is that church as God intended is supposed to be moving. The Kingdom of God is a movement. In all of its best moments, it was a rapidly spreading movement. So all we really need is to go back to what we have always been born to be. There is a divine design within us that will shine especially bright if we can let go of what we once thought was security but was actually a false hope.

In this chapter I will address ways we need to shift our thinking if we hope to gain a footing in this rapidly changing world.

Five paradigm shifts to start moving

The shifts we must make are more than simply a new logo, a new staff member, or a new wing added to our facility. We have to change the way we see things and act immediately on that new knowledge.

1. Lifelong learning is essential

Credentials are not as valued as they once were. It used to be that a few years of education and a certification from an accredited agency would set you up for a lifelong career. In a few fields you would need to update your certification annually, but it would not require much to do so. The social promise of a career following a degree has been broken for many years now. A bachelor's degree is as common now as a high school diploma was thirty years ago. A master's degree is now as common as a bachelor's used to be. Doctorates are becoming commonplace and are not a guarantee of employment in many fields.

Because of the exponential development of technology, credentials can lose relevancy quickly in many fields. By the time a student walks across the stage to graduate, the diploma he receives can already be out-of-date because the field has changed so quickly. This is, of course, worse in some fields than in others, but in all fields, education is less helpful then it once was.

I'm not saying education is of no value and should be jettisoned, but I believe that it doesn't prepare us as it once did and certainly doesn't guarantee a career. We must shift to a different way of understanding education. We need new models of learning.

Thomas L. Friedman surmises, "Another big challenge is the way we educate our population. We go to school for twelve or more years during our childhoods and early adulthoods, and then we're done. But when the pace of change gets this fast, the only way to retain a lifelong working capacity is to engage in lifelong learning."[5]

Learning should be a lifelong adventure, a quest. Only a fool would say that they have learned all that is important and have nothing more to learn. We should always be endeavoring to learn more. God and His Word are infinite, and our hunger for knowledge should never be satisfied this side of heaven.

Expertise is losing value as a currency because the inflation rate is just too high. In many fields, having experience in a previous time may be more detrimental than helpful for the present. If a field has changed dramatically, the one employed may actually cause damage by relying on old skills and information. In such cases it is more expensive to help someone unlearn and then relearn than it is to teach someone new.

In some fields, people are more interested in how you think, process, and adapt to new ideas than in the education, experience, and accumulated knowledge you have in the subject. Today's education is a lifelong pursuit. You don't graduate until there is a flatline on the screen next to your bed.

Some forward-thinking businesses are offering a combination of employment and education to those employees who assess well; this gives them ongoing training and education on the job.[6] They are doing this in lieu of hiring those who have graduated from university. These corporations are producing home-grown employees that are made for their business rather than hiring those trained by an institution that cannot keep up with the field.

Constant learning is a tiring and challenging enterprise, but the good news is that we have access to so much information to improve our skills. With all the access we have to cutting-edge studies on the Internet, we have no excuses for a lack of growth. We can literally improve our understanding and skills every few years. Why not? Don't strive to be learned, but learning.

2. Leadership must be redefined

For far too long, a leader in the Church was defined as a person who sees what is ahead, develops a plan of action, and then casts vision for that preferred future with a group of people who follow him or her.

There are two reasons why this no longer works. First, it was always a bad model because it creates a dependency on human leaders and prevents everyone from hearing from God. Second, our leaders are increasingly unable to predict the future.

A leader is no longer a dependable bridge from the present to the future as we were all taught to believe. A leader must help people be ready for the now. Vision casting is less important than value seeding. There are few leaders who can foresee the specifics of the future these days and prepare people to thrive in it. What we can do is prepare people for any future, rather than cast vision for our own idealized version of it.

This is actually a very good thing. Relying on leaders to climb up the mountain to hear from God and then march back down to cast the vision for all of us to follow is outdated, and it stunts the maturation of the Church.

It is my firm belief that the leaders of tomorrow will be less concerned with finding followers than releasing reproducers. Leadership must become an equipping role that helps all the people become effective in their current environment. The lynchpin leader, who is the center of the organization, is not what we need. What we need is a leader who knows how to get out of the way and be forgotten in the wake of others' successes. The old maxim, "lead, follow, or get out of the way," should now become "lead, follow *and* get out of the way." In fact, the more that each person succeeds, the more we all succeed. Leaders, find a way to make others more valuable than yourself, and that will be your greatest success.

Leadership in a movement is more about influencing influencers than it is about being the one who is the "face" of the Church. For instance, if the vision and direction come from one person and are carried out by others, then there is a dependency that curtails true reproduction. Sound leadership in a movement is not coming up with *the* vision and casting it to others but instead helping others find their own vision of what God wants them to do and then releasing them to the ends of the earth.

Real success for a leader in God's Kingdom is measured by the number of people empowered to discover their own unique calling rather than a large following of people to fulfill one man's vision. A leader is no longer valued by the number of followers he has accumulated, but by the number of leaders that have been developed and deployed around them. Leader, don't consider your role to be producing people who are right, but people who are good. Good people will continue to learn; those who think they are right run the risk of not learning anything new.

An effective leader today must be one who delights more in asking questions than in giving answers. John E. Kelly III, IBM's senior vice president of Cognitive Solutions, once said, "In the twenty-first century, knowing all the answers won't distinguish someone's intelligence—rather, the ability to ask all the right questions will be the mark of true genius."[7] Equipping people to find answers to questions is more helpful than simply being a source of answers for several reasons:

1. Self-discovery and self-directed learning is a deeper and more memorable learning because it is reinforced with auto-biographical memory.

2. People that can find solutions in the absence of the leader are more self-sufficient and have lasting influence.

3. Those who find answers in the context of experience and relationships hold those answers with potential empathy and compassion, making them better people.

4. Personal ownership of solutions can mobilize people to share their discoveries more readily with others.

5. Delving into discovery yields more benefits than simply finding answers and may unearth more important findings than the straightforward solution alone provides.

The type of leader who is the source of all answers became obsolete when Google was launched. If you are a leader in a church, you need to find a way to be influential beyond simply giving people the right answers. Siri fulfills that role now. You must learn to help people ask better questions and pursue deeper ideas.

3. Resources shouldn't be banked: they should be spent while still valuable

Money in the bank and equity in properties once gave us the illusion of stability. Even in the past this was only a seductive lie, but today that lie is increasingly obvious.

I mentioned in chapter three that the middle class in America is no longer the majority. I pointed out that the very rich are increasing their wealth at an exorbitant rate while the poor are also increasing rapidly. As the very rich gain more wealth and the rest of us are dropping lower, the value of money is increasingly in a state of flux. Governments are printing cash to pay debts that are increasing at a rapid rate. Inflation rates will start to rise as more money is printed and unattached to any substantive base like the gold standard of the past. These are not days to horde money or possessions. What God puts in our hands today should be used today, for tomorrow it may not be worth much. Each day, the money we hold loses value, and that depreciation could soon increase at an alarming rate. Don't be caught holding onto something worthless and miss out on grabbing hold of real impact in the present.

The rise in technology also affects this. Items that were once priced for wealthier people see their value drop as next-generation products become available. We are living in days when we need to use whatever resources God has provided now instead of saving them for later.

4. Invest in younger people

All of us reading this book were born during this giant population boom. But the later you were born into it, the more you are accustomed to the effects of it. The younger you are, the more adept you may be at being missional in this environment but also the more blinded to the rapid changes.

We have leaders in the church world who have never matured to the place where they are multiplying themselves. They are still doing the same things they always have, the things that run and manage church programs. When the Church is dependent upon leaders that have plateaued and not matured, then the Church remains immature as well. We need leaders that mature and invest in the next generation. We need leaders more interested in their spiritual children's success than their own success.

If you can sing the theme song to *Gilligan's Island*, you are already at an age where you should be investing in younger people. Don't strive to be relevant, strive to be a resource. That is the true call upon the leader in God's Kingdom.

The millennial generation is adept at swimming in this world of rapid technological change. Generation Z will be even more so. But these are also generations that long for spiritual parenting.

5. Strategic planning must be replaced with strategic people

Gone are the days of going on a retreat to come up with a ten-year plan using sticky notes on a big board. It is virtually impossible to predict what will happen a year from now; ten years might as well be ten light-years.

The Blockbuster Video company probably had a ten-year plan just a few years ago. It's likely collecting dust in someone's drawer as silverfish fodder. Success today is no guarantee of success tomorrow, and believing so is usually a death sentence to your organization. Whatever got you to success now will leave you in the dust if you trust it for your future.

Church, as a whole, has always done better with the past and future than with the present. We tend to look back with fond memories of glory days gone by, "stuck in a moment." We also have a tendency to look forward to a "get-out-of-jail-free" card, with hopes of a rapture to help us escape our present. Both of these perspectives are huge handicaps for today. We can no longer afford to stay stuck in the past awaiting a preferable future; we must awaken to the now and do what we can in this moment. Emily Dickinson's poem is apt: "Forever—is composed of Nows."[8]

So if we cannot plan for the future, what can we do? We can prepare for *any* future. Rather than a strategic plan, what we really need are *strategic people*. We need to be a people who can take advantage of whatever comes our way. We need to prepare people to excel in the now. Joshua Cooper Ramo, in his book *The Age of the Unthinkable*, calls this: "Mastery of the passing instant."[9]

So should we abandon any strategic planning? No, I am not suggesting that. I am suggesting that we hold on to our future plans with light fingers and keep our eyes trained on what is happening now. In fact, the art of strategic planning can help us become better at being strategic people now. The former general and president Dwight D. Eisenhower shed light on this idea when he said, "In preparing for battle, I have always found that plans are useless but planning is indispensable."

Be aware that there are a ton of variables that will impact all our plans that we cannot count on or plan for. So we need to hold loosely to our plans and be prepared to scrap them in an instant. This means we must be less emotionally invested in our vision of the future and more invested in discovering the opportunities found in the present.

More than a meeting

There have been many "Aha!" moments in my life when a realization hits that changes everything. A few years ago I had one such epiphany. Prior to that moment, I had given my life to starting churches that multiplied.

I heard the Lord say to me, "So if you get millions of people meeting together in homes once a week all over the world, do you think that will be enough to change the world?"

It wasn't that starting churches was a bad idea; I am still investing in that. But there is more—so much more—to be done beyond a meeting. The Church is meant to *work* together, not just worship together—in fact, working together *is* worshiping together.

Since that enlightenment I have been a part of starting more than churches. I focus on starting *missional Kingdom outposts*. Yes, these are indeed churches of a sort, but meeting in regularly scheduled Bible studies is not the aim, and often that isn't even what happens.

Is a regularly scheduled meeting a good thing? Of course it can be. A meeting, however, does not make a church, any more than a regularly scheduled meeting is what makes your family a family. Can a church exist without a scheduled meeting? Yes, it can.

There are often no sermons, Sunday schools, or "services," in these

Kingdom outposts, yet the Scriptures are the foundation to all they do. People live and work in community; they don't just hear a message, sing songs, and pass the plate. Often there are no offerings taken, but there is tremendous generosity. The people in these groups share their lives together. They are giving so much more than their time and 10 percent of their treasure to the Kingdom work. These people are giving up their whole being—their sweat, provision, vocation, sense of purpose, and identity—all to Jesus.

I would compare the disciples coming out of these outposts favorably against any coming from traditional church forms. I'm not being boastful, just honest. I have spent time with some followers of Christ from this movement, and they are not like the typical churchgoer. As my associate Dezi Baker says, "They are different enough to make a difference."

You can't produce a world-changing disciple with a one-hour service on Sundays and a Bible study on Wednesday nights. The deluded idea that this is the best way to do our spiritual work is as common as it is unrealistic. Disciples are made in the hard work of real life—in the marketplace, not a meeting place. Our impact should be felt in the populace, not just in the pews. We should measure our influence on the streets, not in the seats.

A promising trend in the Kingdom of God

I have the privilege of traveling around the world equipping people to release Jesus movements. I get to see firsthand what God is doing globally. In the early days of our organic church movement, I would share what we were learning and find God had already been speaking to people everywhere about this same idea. I was often just giving encouragement and descriptive language to what they were already committed to. This is because the Holy Spirit leads His people simultaneously, spontaneously and globally.

This same experience is happening again these days but with this new trend of Kingdom outposts. I run into people in every nation I visit who are putting very similar principles to work. Most people who are practicing these things feel like they are the only ones in the world doing so. When they discover that others are hearing the same thing and that they can learn from experienced people around the world, it is very encouraging and affirming.

This trend I am seeing everywhere is the planting of new works that may be church (in a broader definition) but are so much more than a local church according to our common understanding. Here are eight shared characteristics of these missional Kingdom outposts:

1. They create micro-businesses that employ people who are becoming Kingdom agents in the world and also provide a needed product for the neighborhood. Whereas a local church is often viewed from the outside as a drain upon the community, these outposts actually provide a product or service, or both, to meet needs. If they were to leave, the neighborhood would feel the loss. Job creation is also an important part of the endeavor, especially when the work is helping hurting people to get back on their feet.

2. They involve providing a localized spiritual family in sustainable community (often living in close proximity, together under a single roof, or on a shared property or neighborhood). For these people, church has become so much more than a once-a-week event. This is not a commune that separates itself from the world, but a sustainable community whose members engage with their neighbors. This also means that they all share the work and provision of the community daily.

3. They often practice sustainable farming (even in urban settings) to provide food for the spiritual family and frequently for the neighborhood as well. Hydroponics and community gardens are popping up all over.

4. They often do volunteer work to clean up neighborhoods and serve the community in tangible and often thankless ways. Painting buildings, fixing homes, planting trees, picking up trash, and feeding the homeless are things that are a part of the regular rhythm in these outposts.

5. They often work closely with very marginalized people in their neighborhood and provide a path toward self-sufficient living and Kingdom fruitfulness. They don't just produce converts but reproducible disciples.

6. They are able to change rapidly and start new things whenever the opportunity presents itself. When one type of business ends, another begins...or maybe three.

7. They are beginning to find each other and network on a global scale—which is exciting. Each outpost has some kind of specialty that they can share with the others in trade.

8. One very odd commonality that I cannot explain is that these outposts all seem to involve a particular product: coffee. I get it. I love coffee, but I suspect there is more to it than that because it is a common trait universally. People either grow it, roast it, sell the beans wholesale, or serve coffee in a café.

I can see multiple reasons for these current trends. Here are five reasons I can determine as to why this trend is increasing all over the globe:

1. Reliance on tax-free donations is tenuous in a future that is rapidly becoming hostile to Christianity; many well-established ministries may—and probably will—discover this in an abrupt and sobering moment.

2. The artificial separations of secular and sacred (as well as clergy and laity) are being dissolved. The result will be a global impact of God's people when they are no longer segregated from the world.

3. Sustainable, local, and green enterprise is not just a fad; this is a strong movement that provides a Kingdom opportunity to serve our world and its inhabitants in a responsible manner. We can be healthier and more responsible in our call to care for the planet. Perhaps someday, we can even lead the way.

4. Disciple making on the job and on the streets is far more effective than attempting to do it in two one-hour meetings a week at a church building. This is actually what church should always have

been about. Some of these Kingdom outposts I was describing do not even have a weekly meeting, but the members spend all day, every day serving together. That is more church than any meeting or address can provide. Living and working together in a missional environment can accelerate development of a whole person. People can mature spiritually more rapidly in the crucible of hard work, but also life skills, emotional health, and relational IQ are increased. The disciples produced are strong, self-sustaining, and able to reproduce after their own kind. Jesus lived and walked with His disciples every day.

5. Providing jobs, raising entrepreneurs, and equipping people to prosper is a necessity as we face this rapidly changing world.

It could very well be that in the near future, many church properties, Christian camps, and missionary bases will transition to something similar to this missional Kingdom outpost model.

When someone is a part of this type of endeavor, there is a real sense of belonging and importance. This provides a steady and sustainable environment for the Kingdom to not only survive but thrive in these chaotic days. In the next chapter I will address reasons why this chaotic world should be an advantage to us.

CHAPTER EIGHT

Some Good News: Chaos Ain't So Bad

Life is like riding a bicycle. To keep your balance, you must keep moving.
—Albert Einstein

The future depends on what you do today.
—Mahatma Gandhi

AT THIS POINT, I'm sure many Christian leaders would like for me to say something that reinforces the work they are already doing and how they are doing it. But even if I said as much, sincerely—they probably wouldn't believe it. Such statements would lack all credibility and ring false.

If what we have been doing could reach the masses, *we would have reached them by now.* Our current practices are perfectly designed to get the results we are now seeing. If we want to make any advancement for the Kingdom of God, we will need to courageously let go of old forms and embrace a new way of being and doing church. It is as simple—and difficult—as that.

Good news in the midst of chaos

There is some good news. There are some advantages presented to us in the midst of this global transformation. We can catch and ride the tidal wave of change. Here are a few ideas that can help:

1. Not everything is changing

God is immutable. He doesn't change. Jesus Christ is the same yesterday, today, and forever. His Kingdom is unshakeable. Find your identity, purpose, and calling there.

These words can easily be heard as simply common rhetoric with little real meaning. Why? Because they have been heard so many times that we've become hardened to their importance. The truth, however, is that God doesn't change based on our perception or faith. He remains the same. Our faith adjusts to who He is, not the other way around.

God has never been subject to our small-minded views or contained by our theological boxes and ecclesiological framework. When we assume He is what we want Him to be and then put our faith and hope on this smaller version of Him, we will always end up disappointed as our idols crash to the floor in pieces. God is not in heaven to protect our sense of security in organizations and theological camps. Many will be shocked to find that God is not on their "side" more than others. In fact, we are either on His side or against Him, and that will be the shock of eternity for many.

In a world that is changing so incredibly fast, we must move closer to Him rather than expect Him to bend toward us. He is the stability, not our ambitions, sense of entitlement, and hard work.

True freedom, and peace that surpasses all our plotting, is only found when Jesus is at the center. He doesn't change. He does not bend to the whims of people or the winds of time. If we can truly find our centeredness and subsequent sense of identity in who He is, rather than what we want to be, we will be unshakeable in the wake of these rapidly rising tides.

2. The gospel is still the good news

It doesn't cost a dime to make a disciple—it only costs your life. If we can structure for multiplication, we will be released from dependency upon money, and that's a good thing. "Christ in you is the hope of glory"[1] — and nothing else is. The Church has always been at its best when it has had no budget, no buildings, and no big shots. These coming days may truly be our finest. Only when the gospel is our sole hope will it ever truly be the hope it should be.

3. Not only is the world developing faster, it is becoming flatter

In his book *The World is Flat*, Thomas L. Friedman wrote about the flattening of cultural hierarchy in the twenty-first century because of globalization.[2] It used to be that only the highly educated and privileged could publish their thoughts. Technology has brought down the pyramid of privilege and levelled the playing field so that the world is becoming flat.

Anyone, anywhere can publish anything and have a global voice immediately. There is a whole lot of white noise because of this, so we have to have something interesting to say, say it well, and keep it short. But this also means the avenues for the gospel are increasing at an exponential rate. Each follower of Christ can and should be a difference maker in this bold new world. I am self-publishing this book, my shortest one yet, to take advantage of the trends mentioned in this very book.

4. Social connectivity is making the world smaller

Because of social media, we are also a shrinking world where any two people on the planet are only four degrees of separation from each other.[3] That means that these two people are connected by only four relationship jumps. A few years ago it was six degrees of separation, but due to the increased connectivity of social media, the distance is actually shrinking. We are closer then ever to those who have yet to believe the good news— but we have to be authentic, vulnerable, and available in relationships to make this an advantage. Performance-oriented ministry will not take advantage of this factor. Relationships are the key to global significance. Unfortunately, the Church has not been good at relationships. We should have an advantage there; in fact, we do, if we only tap into the life already within us.

5. The mobility of entire populations presents opportunities

The mass movement of entire populations is opening the door to reach people that once were unreachable. People forced from their homelands are often leaving more than their nation; many are leaving their religions and are open to something more hopeful and kind. Incredible amounts of people are open to the gospel, and they are already apostolic (sent) and now accustomed to being marginalized—they were *sent* before they were *saved*. Imagine the possibilities for this rapidly emerging and fluid mission field full of ready-made missionaries.

6. The power of multiplication can work for us, but we must do things differently

If just one person read this book and decided to take a whole year to make only one disciple in such a way that both he/she and the new disciple could do the same thing the next year, we would be on the path to fulfilling the Great Commission in our generation. If they all continued multiplying like that, within only thirty-six years they will have reached everyone on the planet. As followers of Christ and agents of His Kingdom, we have all that is necessary to fulfill His Great Commission. We can do this, but we can't do it the way we've been trying to do it. It's time to realize that the way we've been doing church isn't going to suddenly start multiplying disciples. We must courageously make changes so that we can multiply, or we risk losing everything much faster than we ever thought we could.

In the next chapter I will explain eight essential core principles necessary for a multiplication movement. All eight characteristics are necessary for true multiplication, and most fly in the face of common church practices.

CHAPTER NINE

Riding the Exponential Waves: Catching Up and Keeping Up

*One of the hardest things for the human mind to grasp
is the power of exponential growth in anything—what happens
when something keeps doubling or tripling or quadrupling over
many years and just how big the numbers can get.*
—Thomas L. Friedman

*Every time we eat, we eat the fruit of God's tremendous reproduction power
given to plants and animals. Look around out of doors; it's everywhere—grass,
trees, birds, bees, babies and flowers. All creation is shouting it! This is the way
God works! ...We ourselves don't make the church grow or reproduce, any more
than pulling on a stalk of corn would make it grow.*
—George Patterson

AMONG THE ITEMS DISPLAYED in the old Museum of Science and Industry in Chicago was a checkerboard with a single grain of rice on the first square, two on the second, four on the third, then 8, 16, 32, 64, 128, and so on. Somewhere down the board, there was enough rice that it was spilling over into neighboring squares, so the display ended there. Above the demonstration was the question: *At this rate of doubling each square, how much rice would you have on the checkerboard by the time you reached the sixty-fourth square?*

To find the answer, you punched a button and the answer flashed on a screen above the board: *Enough to cover the entire subcontinent of India, fifty feet deep.* There would be 153 *billion* tons of rice—more than the world rice harvest for the next one thousand years. Walter Henrichsen, in his book *A Disciple is Made Not Born*, described this scene to illustrate the potent power of multiplication. He went on to conclude, "The reason that the church of Jesus Christ finds it so hard to stay on top of the Great Commission is that the population of the world is multiplying while the church is merely adding. Addition can never keep pace with multiplication."[1] This is absolutely, unforgivingly true.

The final solution is already ours

I once attended a church planting training that taught two "secrets" to church growth. "All you need," said the speaker, "are these two things, and more people will come, more souls will be saved, and your church attendance will shoot up." He paused for dramatic effect, and the antici-pation among wannabe megachurch leaders rose. Finally he told us: "Number one: plenty of parking spaces, and number two: clean bathrooms."

If only we had a larger facility or more parking we would see more people saved and enfolded into our spiritual family, right? That is not only incorrect; it is heresy. There is no "secret" practice or "magic" checklist that if done faithfully will guarantee spiritual results. None. Ever.

There is a final solution, and His name is Jesus. When we place our faith in our practices, we place our dependence on faulty things that will only produce disappointment. Worse yet, we are also not placing our faith in Christ, the only real hope. I believe the latter is the worst part because it nullifies Christ's sacrifice and power, and we end up doing some pretty foolish things in His name but void of His power. There is salvation in no other name but Jesus.

When we place our faith in our methods rather than the good news, we fall off the edge of orthodox doctrine and become stuck in the mire of legalism. Legalism is more than just trying to merit salvation by obeying the Law. Believing that our efforts produce spiritual results and either salvation or spiritual growth is legalistic. Nevertheless, we do so all the time.

I believe we will not truly experience the power of the gospel until we believe in it and only it. When we trust the gospel to do what only it can do, we will discover all it truly can do. As long as we think we can help the gospel out with our slick programs and swank properties, we will get feeble results. We often have a form of godliness void of any real power. Most of the time, all we trust the gospel for is a ticket to heaven when we die. It is capable of so much more than that.

I propose that our greatest mistake in Christendom is that we do not fully grasp the realities of the gospel. Salvation and all it entails is all we need to not just change our lives, but the entire world. A soul saved by the good news of Jesus is so much more than we ever realize. The gospel of Jesus Christ is the final solution to all that ails us—and the world. I firmly believe this and would die for it without hesitation.

Once people have Christ, they have *all* that is necessary. They are blessed with every spiritual blessing in the heavenly places (Ephesians 1:3). They already have all that is needed to be godly in Christ (2 Peter 1:3). All authority in heaven and earth is with them, always (Matthew 28:19-20; Hebrews 13:5). All the righteousness of Christ is transferred to their account, and all their sin and evil is paid for in full and can never dampen their soul again (2 Corinthians 5:21). The Holy Spirit takes up residence within the regenerate soul and becomes the source of all goodness (Galatians 5:22-23).

The idea that our ministry in church can add anything to all the above is, frankly, insane. It is a devious lie that diminishes the work of Christ and replaces it with a hollow promise of growth—but in the end, the only thing that truly grows is our ego. Within the Christ-follower is all that is necessary to catalyze gospel movements. A potent chain reaction of changed lives is a result of releasing the good news of Jesus on a broken and unsuspecting world. If none of this is true and I am deceived, then it would be better to just die. Trying to accomplish the objectives of faith without the gospel would be a living nightmare…it would be church as we have known it.

Adding anything to the gospel doesn't just diminish the fruit—it destroys it. Christ supplemented is Christ supplanted. The true goal of a godly leader is not to put good stuff in people, but to let the God stuff out. That is what it means to be an equipper of others. Unfortunately we believe too often that "my teaching," "this new program," or "a better curriculum" will bring about godly character and produce spiritual growth in people. That is a heresy of the highest order.

When we say we believe in the gospel and then go about doing ministry as though we need to help it along, we put faith in ourselves and not in Christ. Ours is not a weak gospel. A gospel that needs our help is no gospel at all. There is nothing we can add to the work of Christ. Nothing.

The secret to a multiplication movement is within every Christ-follower, no matter how old they are, what status they have, or what training they have received. A brand new believer has the same amount of spiritual power as the most mature.

By spiritual power, I mean the salvation of Christ, which grants a person complete access to God and everything necessary to live a godly life, bear fruit, and fulfill one's life calling. This is not the same thing as wisdom or maturity, which requires both experience and time. Wisdom and experience do not grant the follower more spiritual power but simply help him or her to realize the power they already have gained in Christ.

Doing good works over a prolonged time does not add anything to the power transferred into our spiritual account from the beginning. Maturity can result from walking with Christ over the years, but not more spiritual potency. Spiritual maturity is simply realizing what we already have—who we already are in Christ—and placing more faith in the simplicity of Christ in us. Christ in us is the hope of glory. We must stop putting all our hope in other things that will fail us.

This concept is counterintuitive and hard for us to accept. This is what is called "the stumbling block of the cross," because we want to believe that we are better than we actually are—and we think we are certainly better than others.

A five-year-old African-American girl in an impoverished neighborhood without any education who only chose to believe in Jesus today is as powerful in the gospel as a mature Christian who has written dozens of books and travels the world teaching others. In the Kingdom of God, the last is first and the first is last. We are all tied in the spiritual race that is faith. No person is more "anointed" than another. No one gets more Holy Spirit than any other. Someone "full of the Spirit" doesn't have more Holy Spirit than any other Christ-follower; that is a dangerous misunderstanding. The real question is, how much of us does the Holy Spirit get? Maturity is simply allowing the Spirit to have more of our will with less resistance. But that doesn't add to the spiritual properties we have in Christ or elevate us in spiritual power or position. It only allows that inherent power to flow more freely.

In essence, our "ministry" is simply to allow Christ to operate more freely through us and others. We no longer have to ask Him to come and give us more. He has already given everything He has. It is more about us giving Him everything we have. We mature the more we yield to Him, but we do not gain any more salvation, power, or spiritual life. That is settled and sealed from the beginning.

This concept is foundational to a multiplication movement that empowers all and spreads from one soul to another freely. We are not seeing a gospel movement, because we are so confused on what the basics are: the gospel, salvation and how a believer grows in Christ. This is no minor mistake.

A paradox with our programs

In review, the power of a multiplication movement is within every one of us who choose to follow Christ. There is, however, a paradox within much of current church methodology that must be explained. While our methods are ineffective for producing spiritual results, they can be potent at preventing spiritual fruitfulness. Our programs are powerless to produce movements, but powerful at *preventing* them. That is the paradox.

I watched as former NBA basketball greats teased each other as commentators on TNT. They bantered back and forth about what a coach can and cannot do for a player. Kenny "The Jet" Smith said, "A coach can't give confidence to a player, but he can take it away." In the same way, our programs cannot cause a gospel movement, but they can stop it.

If the potential of a gospel movement is already present in each of us, it is not so much that we need to figure out how to make it happen, but instead to stop doing whatever is preventing it from happening.

In other words, it isn't that we lack models, funding, strategy, leadership, or doctrine. By investing so much confidence in those things instead of in the gospel itself, we are unintentionally choking the movement and not simply releasing what Christ has already put in us. Could it be that we are holding back a real movement while all the time searching for one? I have come to believe this is true, and it is slowly killing us.

Our mission is to release the power of the gospel from one life to another in such a way that it multiplies and spreads like a virus from our neighborhoods to the nations. It might sound strange when you read this, but I believe it takes much more effort to prevent multiplication movements than to see them happen. It is harder to not multiply than it is to multiply. This is counterintuitive, but true nonetheless. The gospel should spread naturally and powerfully without our help—and leave in its wake transforming agents of the Kingdom.

I also believe that a true multiplication movement of the gospel is much less expensive than all our efforts that end up preventing it from happening in the first place. We could save a lot of money and energy and see much more effective results if we shift to a new way of seeing the mission accomplished.

Because addition may produce faster results in the beginning and multiplication takes time, we are often content with growth by addition. We choose the more immediate success and gratification of addition instead of waiting for the momentum that can build with multiplying. We have an addition addiction. Don't be content with addition. Stop applauding the pathetic success we see in addition and start longing for the incredible power of multiplication. This would mean, in practical terms, to not look for immediate or large results in the early days. Christian leaders would need to invest in the few rather than in the multitudes, much like Jesus did. Authority would be distributed and decentralized. Growth would need to come from each disciple rather than from a single leader or strong personality. As leaders, we would need to think of ways to equip people to serve rather than simply serving people.

We cannot simply tack on multiplication strategies to our current addition practices, because each set has completely different requirements. Addition is accumulative and draws people in. Multiplication is distributive and sends people out. The objectives and means of accomplishing each are contrary to the other. You cannot do them both at the same time, any more than you can suck in water through a straw and blow bubbles in the glass at the same time. We must stop adding if we want to start multiplying. Could it be that our commitment to strategies that cannot multiply is in fact what is keeping us from seeing a movement here in the West? I do believe this is true, and it is costing us so much more than we can imagine.

Eight essential qualities of a multiplication movement

Every one of these qualities is necessary if we are to see real multiplication. None can be violated and still result in a multiplication movement.

You will find that most of these principles are counterintuitive. This is how real multiplication movements work.

1. Slow and small wins the race

Multiplication by doubling begins slower than addition, but like a car rolling down a steep hill, it builds up momentum as it goes. A penny doubled, then doubled again can become millions, and then billions, and within a short time, trillions. In fact, you go from billions to trillions just as fast as you went from millions to billions. This is phenomenal.

This first principle is one of the hardest for missionaries and church planters to grasp because it counters all their intuition and plans. The vast majority of church planters long for their church to quickly grow large. Launching large is seen as the most viable way to success for the church planter these days. Church planting agencies are actually guilty of stopping any multiplication before it can start because, as I will explain, movements are most vulnerable to being stopped at the very beginning. Church planter salaries frequently are set up so that they decrease significantly each year, hoping that will provide motivation for them to launch big enough to make up the difference through the offerings collected in the new worship service. A church planter is forced to launch larger in the beginning just to support his or her family. A gathering of people in a worship service that can contribute tithes and offerings has become the main objective for a church planter. This takes precedence over reproducing disciples or bringing life and change to a community. Our systems are designed to prevent multiplication from the very start. These same systems also work overtime to make one leader key to the whole enterprise and limit church to what happens on Sunday morning between the hours of 10 o'clock and noon.

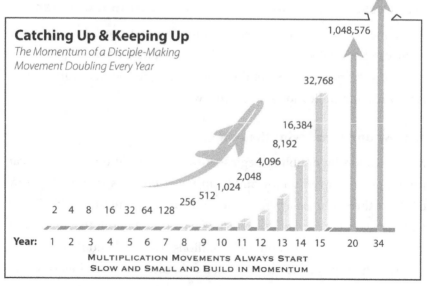

Figure 9.1

We simply must respect the long runway necessary for this movement to take off. We should allow this long, slow start to be part of the plan and expect it. Instead, when we hit the long, slow start, we lose patience, feel like we are failing, and resort to addition practices. When we shift from multiplication to addition, we disrupt the natural flow of momentum that would eventually overtake all else. We may feel more successful in the early days with addition, but we forfeit the ideal results that come through multiplication.

Patience is not just a virtue in multiplication—it's a necessity. Just as a farmer cannot quicken the growth of his crops, the church planter who wants multiplication results must be willing to wait. "The farmer waits for the precious produce of the soil, being patient about it, until it gets the early and late rains. You too be patient; strengthen your hearts, for the coming of the Lord is near" (James 5:7-8). Paul said that we will reap what we have sown *in due time*—if we do not give up (Galatians 6:7-9).

Steven Covey asked: "Did you ever consider how ridiculous it would be to try to cram on a farm—to forget to plant in the spring, play all summer and then cram in the fall to bring in the harvest?" He went on, "The farm is a natural system. The price must be paid and the process followed. You always reap what you sow; there is no shortcut."[2] There are seasons. We must "be ready in season and out" and not rush the process.

The Bible is not silent on this. Do not "despise these small beginnings" (Zechariah 4:10 NLT). A tiny mustard seed of faith is all that is needed to move mountains (Matthew 17:20). A pinch of leaven is all that is needed to leaven the whole lump (Galatians 5:9). Every person that is changed by Jesus can be a carrier of the movement, and multiplication starts there. This leads us to the next essential principle of multiplication.

2. Each one reach one

Some argue that multiplication requires addition, and that is true. We cannot multiply without addition, but we certainly can add without multiplying. Multiplication, in the Kingdom sense of the word, only works if each one that is added, adds another, then another. This highlights the big difference between addition and multiplication. The difference is seen in the multiple generations.

In multiplication, each person is equally important to the process, so there isn't an outstanding personality that can produce more of it than everyone else.[3] Everyone gets to play in a multiplication movement—that is the only way to have one.

How we start will determine how we finish. Once our entire system is set up to only add, multiplying becomes impossible. In a multiplication movement, each one must reach one, again and again, for many generations. Only when everyone is empowered, and each generation is being discipled and reproducing disciples, can a multiplication movement happen.

Everyone is the hero of a multiplication movement, and no single person stands out as the sole leader. Perhaps this is because in a real Jesus movement, Jesus gets the attention and affection of those involved rather than any human leader.

3. Break the Gen-4 barrier

I believe the proof of multiplication is found in the fourth generation. 2 Timothy 2:2 is the key verse about multiplying disciples in the New Testament.

> And the things you [Timothy] have heard me [Paul] say in the presence of many witnesses entrust to reliable people [third generation] who will also be qualified to teach others [fourth generation and beyond].
> 2 TIMOTHY 2:2 NIV

In this verse we see *four* generations of reproduction: Paul, Timothy, reliable people, and others. "Others" represents more than just a fourth generation—it includes every generation thereafter. Once we pass the fourth generation, the momentum kicks in and succeeding generations don't just become possible, but probable.

A strong leader will attract other leaders, who, because they are leaders, will have followers. In that sense, we can have three generations via addition. But to see the fourth generation, we must be doing things differently—we must be giving it all away to get through the barrier between addition and multiplication. We should hold this marker up as our scorecard of success more than the numbers that are in attendance. Once we break through the Gen-4 barrier, multiplication has a momentum of its own. It is also beyond anyone's control. What can possibly spread from one life to another past these four generations? That question leads us to the next essential principle of multiplication.

4. The gospel glue

In his seminal book *The Tipping Point*, Malcolm Gladwell introduced an idea that was so descriptive and helpful that it "stuck" with me. He called it the "stickiness factor." His terminology became sticky itself as more people began to use the phrase.[4]

The stickiness factor has to do with the memorable quality of the idea, product, or method that is spread in a movement. When the idea is so intriguing that it sticks with people enough that they *can't* forget about it, a movement can happen. This is (pardon the pun) the glue that makes a movement come together. You can sell products, ideas, and even ministries with advertising and mass media promotion, but that is not a movement. To ignite a true movement, the idea *itself* must spread from one person to another—and only sticky ideas can do that.

I believe that anything less than a Jesus movement—where lives are changed by the good news of Jesus and that transformation spreads to others—is not worthy of His name. When someone is transformed from the inside out by the indwelling presence of the Spirit of Jesus, that person cannot help but tell others. That is stickiness unlike any other.

Jesus is more than any brand of church or ministry. We would be surprised what people will do for Jesus that they will not do for our church vision statement and brand. Frankly, if the gospel doesn't drastically change lives, what is the point of church? It's better to just eat, drink, and be merry, for tomorrow we all die. But I do believe the gospel is a spark that can ignite a fast-spreading wildfire that cannot be put out by man, demon, or even Satan himself. I believe that Jesus changes lives—He changed mine—so I will spread that news for the rest of my days.

Christ in us is the hope of glory. That is the stickiness of the gospel. This hope expressed through us in our changed lives is the contagion of the gospel. Anything else is less than a Kingdom movement. This, in and of itself, is something worth giving our lives to—and giving our lives for.

The contagion, however, needs to spread from one life to another, which brings us to the next principle necessary for a multiplication movement. It doesn't matter how sticky our message is if we don't have the tracks for the movement to roll forward on and expand.

5. Multiplication runs on relationships

The gospel spreads best on the tracks of relationships. A quick survey of any Christian audience will bear this truth out. Ask how many people came to Christ anonymously, and one or two people in the crowd will raise their hands. All the others will raise their hands when asked how many came to Christ through an important relationship with a trusted friend or family member.

This is the design of God. We are made to be in relationship, and that is the context for lives to change. The term used in the Gospels to describe this is the word *oikos*, most often translated as "household" (referring to a set of familial relationships). Jesus' instructions were to enter into a household with the gospel and stay there, letting the gospel spread from one relationship to another. Jesus instructed the apostles—and us—about extending the gospel of the Kingdom with the following words:

> *"When you enter a house [oikos] first say, 'Peace be to this house [oikos].' If someone who promotes peace is there, your peace will rest on them; if not, it will return to you. Stay there, [oikos],*

eating and drinking whatever they give you; for the worker deserves his wages. Do not move around from house [oikos] to house [oikos]."
LUKE 10:5-7 NIV

Five times in the above verses, Jesus used the word *oikos* (household), emphasizing that relationships are the key to gospel extension. In fact, He goes so far as to instruct us to not greet people with our message (gospel) of peace (*shalom*) on the way (Luke 10:4). In other words, don't evangelize void of the context of real, authentic, and vulnerable relationships. Why? He wants more than simply adding converts to the membership rolls in heaven. He wants nothing less than a radically multiplying, life-changing movement of the gospel that starts and spreads with *oikos* relationships.

I want to point out that the last command from Jesus in the passage above is in the imperative voice: "*Do not* move around from house to house." Wait, uh, what? Yeah, He commands us to not go to the next household. Doesn't Jesus want the gospel to spread from house to house? Yes, He does, but He doesn't want you to do it all. He wants it to spread from one satisfied, saved and sanctified "recipient" to the next. He wants a true movement. Relationships have always been the tracks that the gospel is meant to move forward on.

For a locomotive to work, you need at least three components:

1. *The locomotive*
2. *The tracks for it to run on*
3. *The energy to make it move*

In a similar way, we need three parts to see a multiplication movement spread:

1. *The message of the gospel (locomotive)*
2. *Connective relationships with hurting people who need the message (tracks)*
3. *Lives that have been changed by the power of the gospel (energy pushing the movement forward)*

We are too often lacking one or more of these elements and so miss all chances of a multiplication movement. We may believe that the gospel is salvation in Christ by grace through faith alone—but then we act as though it is our own effort and good works that make a difference. And then we have something less than a train. If we are only moral people—"cultural Christians"—rather than true, vibrant carriers of the gospel, then we lack any energy to propel the movement. But the middle element is also frequently missing. Most Christians have good relationships with other Christians but do not have strong connections with those who need the gospel most. We have no tracks for the movement to run forward on. A train full of steam but without tracks to run on is utterly useless.

Once someone is a Christian for longer than six months, most of their meaningful relationships are with other Christians. Their connections and friendships with people in the lost and broken world are cold and dead. If the gospel of the Kingdom spreads along the lines of an *oikos* connection and their entire *oikos* is already Christian, then any potential movement is derailed.

I often say, "If we want to win this world to Christ, we're going to have to sit in the smoking section." We simply must create avenues for the gospel to flow from relationship to relationship.

Even in the best of circumstances, this barricade to movements exists simply because a new life in Christ will be attracted to a spiritual family of like-minded people. Christ-followers, by divine design, long to be in fellowship with other followers of Christ. It is an internal and natural intent, which means that for most people, the days soonest after their rebirth may be their most productive for extending the movement from *oikos* to *oikos*. As time passes, it is less natural and more challenging to bridge into an *oikos* that needs the gospel.

Believing that a new spiritual life is too fragile to carry the gospel contagion and withstand the temptations of the world, we intentionally erect a barrier when people come to Christ. We extract them from mean-ingful relational opportunities and encourage them to solely connect with other believers. This is, once again, misplaced faith that actually puts more confidence in the power of darkness than light. No matter

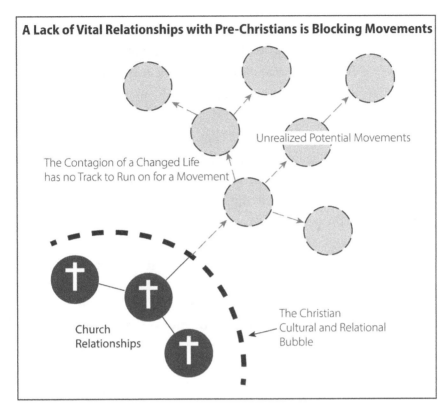

A Lack of Vital Relationships with Pre-Christians is Blocking Movements

Unrealized Potential Movements

The Contagion of a Changed Life
has no Track to Run on for a Movement

Church
Relationships

The Christian
Cultural and Relational
Bubble

Figure 9.2

what we say, we demonstrate by our actions that we believe our own methods and practices are better at protecting a new believer than the gospel, so we do all we can to protect them. We end up only protecting the unsuspecting world from the power of the gospel.

Not only is a new follower of Christ capable of withstanding the temptations of the old life, she is often better suited to make a difference than an older and more mature brother or sister. Why? The fresh relationship lines connect the changing life to those who are in most need of it. The tangible realities of the gospel transformation are most noticeable to these not-yet-believers because they watch their friend change right before their eyes.

Perhaps the most embarrassing truth about this misinformed practice of withdrawing a new convert from his old relationships in an attempt to strengthen the new believer is that in doing this, we actually slow the growth and maturity of the new disciple. Nothing will accelerate a follower of Christ's spiritual development like telling others the good news. In fact, the more hostile the audience, the more the new believer will grow spiritually as they defend the gospel and practice obedience against hostility. Strength is best developed against resistance.

By "protecting" the new believer from the temptations of their old life and friends' lifestyle, we unintentionally collude with the enemy in stopping movements before they happen. We stunt the growth and development of the new disciple as well.

The core truth of the gospel is love. Love is impossible void of relationships. Relationships with those who most need such love is key to the advancement of movements.

6. Multiplication movements are most vulnerable at the beginning

To better understand the momentum behind multiplication movements, imagine a car without gasoline on top of a steep hill. Gasoline is not important in such a case because gravity itself can propel the vehicle. But the ground is almost flat at the top of the hill. Gravity is not tugging at the car immediately. We could simply stand in front of the two-ton car with our hand on the hood and hold it in place. Why? There is no energy behind the car—yet.

This reveals a very important principle for us: movements are most vulnerable at the start. Once the car starts rolling down the hill, its energy increases, and the car moves faster with every inch. Gravity does its work. The acceleration increases rapidly as the car rolls further down the hill. Standing in front of the car and placing your hand on the hood when it is halfway down the steep hill will not slow the car at all—and will probably leave a grease spot on the road.

Movements are much harder to stop once the momentum kicks in, but before that, movements can be easily derailed.

As I stated firmly, the power of movements is found within every

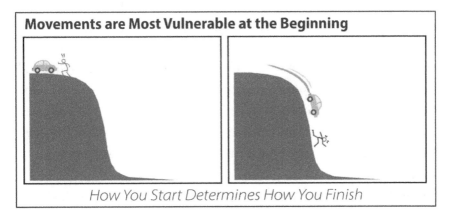

Movements are Most Vulnerable at the Beginning

How You Start Determines How You Finish

Figure 9.3

Christ-follower. If this is true, then why do we not see more movements? This principle answers that question. The movements we could potentially see are stopped before they ever get started.

I contend that the very way we practice our faith and live in community works against multiplication movements. We create dependency on expert leaders from the very start. We frequently cut off the potential power and connection of every new Christ-follower at the very beginning. We make church bound to a physical address and a weekly schedule. All of these things work together to curtail movements right at the start. How we start will determine how we finish. If we want the rapid exponential growth curve at the end, we must lay the groundwork for it in the beginning.

7. Multiplication is simple and significant

As an art student in university, I learned a valuable lesson that I have integrated into all I do: Less is more. The best things are simple things.

We are often tempted to disregard simple things, believing them to be simplistic. A simple thing, however, can be very profound. In fact, I believe that simplicity can be a step *beyond* complexity. What is easy is often simple, but simple is not always easy. It takes great skill and effort to make something simple. It is easy to create something that is complex; we just keep adding "stuff" to it. To design something that is *both* simple and profound, however, is a creative challenge.

Simple is transferable, while complex breaks down. Three of the most feared words in a parent's vocabulary are, "Some assembly required." Inevitably, the more complicated toys break almost immediately. One Christmas I brought home a large box for my five-year-old daughter. The box contained an entire house—a child's toy playhouse. I opened the box with trepidation, but the first thing I noticed was there were no small parts, nuts, or bolts—just the large heavy-duty plastic pieces. I then opened the instructions that were surprisingly simple. They were simple diagrams without words in any language.

I looked for a list of the tools I would need to construct this house, but there was no such list. This was a wonderful toy. The house was put together like a huge three-dimensional puzzle in which all the pieces snap together. Simple. That toy lasted years after our three children's interest in it did. The designers who engineered that toy impressed me. They understood children and their parents and created something that was simple, enjoyable, and virtually indestructible.

When we approach disciple making with the desire to pass the baton on to succeeding generations, we must refine the process so that it is simple and transferable. Simplicity is the key to the fulfillment of the Great Commission in this generation. If the process is complex, it will break down early in the transfer to the next generation of disciples. The more complex the process is, the greater the giftedness needed to keep it going.

Paul passed on to Timothy truths so profound that he would not forget them. They gripped his life and never left him. But the things Paul passed on were simple enough that Timothy could in turn pass them on to others who could then pass them on to more. The gospel itself is the most profound truth mankind has ever received, yet it is simple enough for a child to understand and pass on to others.

Perhaps the reason we don't see multiplication of disciples more often is that we are trying to do too much too soon in the process. We fail to grasp the fact that discipleship—following Christ in simple obedience—

is a lifelong pursuit. By attempting to teach our disciples so much in the first year, we unintentionally sabotage the years to follow. We intimidate them into thinking disciple making is too hard for common people to do and requires memorization of volumes of information. We tend to overestimate what we can do in one year and underestimate what we can do in three. A helpful idea is for us to see disciple making and multiplying as distinct from the process of mentoring leaders. All Christians are to be disciple makers, even those who are not yet leaders.

When we try to combine discipleship with leadership development, we eliminate a good percentage of Christians from participation in the Great Commission. In reality, disciple making is the foundation of good mentoring and leadership development. If we allow disciple making to happen, unencumbered by complicated training methods, more people will be able to do it, and we will increase the pool to draw from for the purpose of mentoring leaders. Once we have growing and multiplying disciples, we can build upon their emerging fruitfulness with intentional mentoring and training methods for those who demonstrate leadership potential.

What we need is a disciple-making system that is practical and profound. It must be both simple and significant: a system that is significant enough to captivate the Christ-follower's internal motivation yet simple enough that it can be easily passed on from disciple to disciple. Such a system will strengthen the Church and produce growth that is qualitative and quantitative.

We cannot easily pass on something complicated from one person to another and then another and so on. The more complex an idea is, the more people will think they are incapable of mastering it. As a result, they will not be empowered to tell others for fear of getting it wrong. A method that is complex is more likely to lose essential elements as it's transferred to upcoming generations.

Simplicity, however, is not just about being able to pass something on. There is more to it. There is something powerful about the refining process that creates a simple and yet potent concept. An idea becomes potent not just from the things we exclude, but also from what we deem so significant that it must remain. Ruthless and relentless prioritizing of an idea refines it.

This process of relentlessly prioritizing and pruning a concept solidifies it into something so important that it cannot be ignored. Seth Godin articulates this when he says, "The art of leadership is understanding what you can't compromise on."[5] Antoine de Saint-Exupéry, best known as the author of *The Little Prince*, once quipped, "Perfection is achieved, not when there is nothing more to add, but when there is nothing left to take away."[6]

Reduction to the most essential and simple points is tricky but worth it. Albert Einstein compelled others to go as close to the edge as possible without letting the idea lose its potency. He said, "Everything must be made as simple as possible. But not simpler."

To take something valuable and reduce it to what makes it valued by eliminating anything that might compete with its significance—and leaving it there—is an incredibly important skill.

Sanity is knowing what to fight for. Insanity is fighting for anything. Cowardice is not fighting for anything. Some things are worth fighting for. Some things are even worth losing a fight over. A few things are worth dying for. I'm convinced that we are ready to lead when we are able to know the things that are worth dying for—and the things not worth fighting over. I believe we will find that after we have lived enough to know these things, more people will receive our message. Our authority increases as we realize this is what we know to be true, and all else becomes secondary.

8. Multiplication is easy and economical

Perhaps the most counterintuitive principle of them all is this: true multiplication is really easy. We are so accustomed to the hard work and sweat of doing ministry that we cannot believe such a thing, but it is true.

In a multiplication movement, everyone does the work, not just a few. The work is narrowed to focus on what is truly important and lesser distractions that cost so much energy are eliminated. All the effort is decentralized and shared. As each one reaches another, the work of the Kingdom is spread to all and no longer rises and falls on a few leaders that do all the heavy lifting.

Jesus described the growth and work of His Kingdom with the following parable:

> "The kingdom of God is like a man who casts seed upon the soil; and he goes to bed at night and gets up by day, and the seed sprouts and grows—how, he himself does not know. The soil produces crops by itself; first the blade, then the head, then the mature grain in the head. But when the crop permits, he immediately puts in the sickle, because the harvest has come."
> MARK 4:26-29

When we all share the load, it becomes easy. In the parable, the farmer doesn't even know how it works. The work grows all by itself. This is something we all can do, should do, and I believe we will do. We just need to stop doing all the other stuff that takes up too much time, too much effort, and too much money—and yields but a tiny fraction of the fruit.

Multiplication is also far less expensive. When the ministry is simplified to what is most powerful and transferable to all, then it suddenly costs next to nothing monetarily. As we often say in our movement, "It doesn't cost a dime to make a disciple—it just costs your life." Jesus paid the ultimate cost for His Kingdom movement; it shouldn't cost more than what He already paid.

Is it possible that we could catch up with the world population and keep up without spending a fortune and killing ourselves in stressful effort in the process? Yes. It is very simple and completely doable. We would only have to focus on doing the very thing Jesus commanded us to do—make disciples.

If we all simply made one disciple every year that could make another the following year, we would not only catch up and keep up—we'd finish up. But to do that, we would have to stop doing a lot of things that set up a few people with power, position, and steady employment.

Virtually all of our "religious" systems are designed to keep power and productivity in the hands of a few professionals. This must change. The next chapter addresses a change to our church operating system.

CHAPTER TEN

Finding Better Ways: Upgrading Our Operating System

There is no magic in small plans. When I consider my ministry,
I think of the world. Anything less than that would not
be worthy of Christ nor of His will for my life.
—Henrietta C. Mears

The clergy must keep the people in ignorance. If they didn't,
the Gospels are so simple that everyone would tell them,
"We understand all this quite well without you."
—Charles-Louis Montesquieu

IN A CHURCH LOBBY, full of Christian leaders milling about booths displaying church growth wares, I ran into an old mentor of mine. We were at a large church planting conference, and after a moment of exchanging pleasantries, he pulled me aside and asked me directly, "Neil, I have to ask you, are you against the Church?"

After a moment of silence and shock, I answered, "No." Then I managed to add, "The word *church* occurs in the title of five of my books." I shifted to face him squarely and said, "You know me, how could you ask such a thing? I've given my life to helping the Church."

He smiled while nodding and said, "That's what I thought." Then he explained, "I just recommended one of your books to fill a need in a church planting organization, and they rejected it saying, 'Neil Cole is against the Church.'"

This is one accusation I get frequently, but it is entirely false. I repeat: *I. Am. Not. Against. The. Church.* That doesn't mean that I do not have corrective things to say to the Church. In fact, it is my love for the Church that compels me to write what I write and say what I say. I've given my life to the Church, for better or worse, until death do us part.

Many of the ways "church" is done are cemented in our psyche so deeply that the *method* used within "church" has become the entity itself. In other words, a Sunday service is "church." A building with a pulpit and pews is "church." In fact, Webster's dictionary has solidified the building as a definition of "church." It's official. My calling is to bring our understanding of "church" into the light and scrutiny of Scripture, not Webster.

There are many denominations and factions in Christianity that hold certain traditions, creeds, and doctrines to be at least as authoritative as Scripture. I cannot argue with them about these things—that choice is their prerogative. Unfortunately, it often doesn't stay there. Leaders who believe church tradition is equally authoritative as the Bible usually go further and claim their own traditions to be biblical. I have the right to question the truthfulness of their assertions when those leaders cling to these traditions with the claim that they are "biblical." And I will.

Are all the old ways the best ways?

One of the mentalities that I rail against is the idea that a single way of doing things— especially one that has been used for hundreds of years—is *the* best way or even the *only* way. Just because it worked in the sixteenth century doesn't mean we cannot find a better way now. In fact, the entire premise of this book is that the old ways of doing ministry are not adequate for this time and are now blocking our discovery of what will work.

It's ridiculous when methodology becomes so fused with the desired objective that anyone not practicing that method is accused of being against the desired outcome. This is how I ended up having a reputation for being "against the Church." Not surprisingly, those who criticize new ways are often the ones who profit most by maintaining the old.

Questioning the status quo does not necessarily mean that we are against the core reason that motivates people to do things the way they have done them. In fact, it could be quite the opposite. If we truly believe in the core reason behind the method, finding a better way would actually mean we care more about it, not less.

Is there a better way for people to learn theology, develop leadership skills, and be a spiritual family together than the current prevailing means that rely on academic achievement and which costs thousands of dollars and takes years to complete? The overwhelming answer is yes. There are better ways. We can certainly innovate and engineer better ways. Not just sufficient ways, but actually *better* ways.

Later in this chapter you will see that we can devise other means to address legitimate needs and not continue to perpetuate systems and institutions that were out-of-date centuries ago. Here are some important things to consider as we approach any spiritual development process that we intend to be fruitful and multiply.

Ten characteristics found in systems that multiply into movements:

1. Self-directed learning

There is voluminous evidence, spanning millennia, that self-directed learning is by far the deepest level of learning. What we discover for ourselves is lodged in our memory as more than just facts—it becomes a part of our story and is kept in the more secure vault of autobiographical memory. We don't just learn a concept, but we remember how we came to know it and why. The stuff learned this way is not pre-processed through some expert's thinking and experience. Instead, it is learned from walking with God and is therefore more authoritative in our lives.

When we devise a method to teach or train people, we should strive to tap into the best kind of learning possible—self-directed study. Why not make that a foundational component of any system of learning? I suggest we talk more about "learning systems" than "teaching curriculum." I know that is semantics, but we should emphasize the people who are doing the learning more than we do those who do the teaching.

Asking good questions is key to facilitating self-directed learning. I often point out that the person who asks the most questions in the Bible is the only one who has all the answers—God. You don't have to go very far to see the questions pouring out of God's mouth. "Adam, where are you?" "Who told you that you are naked?" "Did you eat of the fruit I told you not to eat?" (Genesis 3)

Why does God ask so many questions? He is soliciting self-awareness and an awakening to God Himself because that is the way a life changes. He wants Adam to own the truth for himself so deeply that the lesson will forever be remembered and applied. Jesus also asked a lot of questions. In fact, He often answered a question with another question.

When we design an operating system that is to help people grow and multiply, both self-discovery and self-directed learning is key. We want people who own for themselves the truth of the gospel so that they will give their lives to it. They will not give their lives to someone else's idea. It is only through self-directed learning that people are passionate enough to become constant and effective evangelists for the message. The message must be theirs if we want them to pass it on. The story must be their own.

2. Learning in community

As we think about learning systems to employ in the Kingdom of God, another concept we should always keep in mind is learning in the context of relationships. Learning is deeper when we learn in community.

Why is that? We can sharpen one another's thought processes. What we are together is better than what we are as individuals, even when added up. The group is more than the sum of its parts. The synergy that is created by wrestling together with an issue cannot be underestimated and cannot be attained by someone alone.

Diverse points of view, varying personalities, and unique perspectives can make the thought process fuller and more meaningful to life. Lesser ideas are challenged and dropped in exchange for more robust ones. There is also the greater potential of accountability for what is learned and even an environment to put those lessons into practice.

3. Simple and replicable methods

Under the guidance of the Holy Spirit, we need to engineer systems and methods that can be transferred from person to person by being sketched on a napkin in five minutes while sitting in a café. In fact, our very best replicable systems pass that test.

If the way we develop people spiritually requires volumes of curricula and years of study, then I suspect we are overcomplicating things. If experts are required to develop the few that can afford the process, it is too cumbersome to multiply. If the accumulation of knowledge is the goal, and we go about naively believing that knowledge is enough to mature people, than our operating system is insufficient to change a person, let alone the world. It is far better to have several simple solutions that release and encourage people to learn for themselves and to pass on what they learn, than it is to continue teaching people who are not moving in obedience.

4. Letting God's Word speak for itself

One consistent and global fault of religious leaders is that we tend to get between God's written Word and the people who need it by adding our own thoughts. We help the Scriptures out with our interpretation and application. Actually, we usually just cloud things up with our own self-importance and create an environment where people do not trust themselves to read, understand, and apply the Word of God—because we don't.

How did we, as followers of Jesus, get to the place where we think God's Word needs us, rather than the other way around? Truthfully, the Word of God suffers more under the abuse of well-intentioned Christian leaders than it ever did under ordinary Christians just trying to obey it. More cults are started by Christian leaders with character flaws than by ordinary Christ-followers who just take God's word and run with it.

We need to release everyone to hear from God without a middleman. In fact, I think all our people would grow much more if we stopped being their teachers and released them to learn and then immediately start sharing with others. Good teaching will be far more helpful to those already moving forward in obedience and who are learning from the Scriptures themselves. In fact, they won't tolerate anything but good teaching.

5. Cost-effective ministry

The way we currently do ministry is just too expensive. What if we could do it better and in ways that cost next to nothing? Would we do that even if it meant the institutions that provide Christian leaders with security and importance would be less necessary?

While I am less optimistic that most leaders will let this happen than I once was, I am sure of one thing—we can develop spiritual people for far less money and see multiplied fruitfulness well beyond our current systems. It won't cost much—just your life.

6. Empowering all God's people in a lateral leadership model

Currently, everything that happens in the institutional church requires a certain amount of specialized knowledge and skill. We are leader dependent and leader deprived at the same time. Christian ministry is engineered to need specialized leadership and so creates a need which is only fulfilled with its own product—it's a vicious circle. We will never have enough leaders to do all we have designed ministry to do.

The vast majority of ministry endeavor in the Western church does two things simultaneously. First, it creates a dependency on leaders. And then it exalts leadership above the people until it results in a separation of clergy and laity—which is against the clear directives of the New Testament.

When we read the New Testament, we have a tendency to read our own biases and worldviews into it. We do this especially when we see any words that represent leadership. A leader in the New Testament is not referred to as "above" but "in front of." You likely pictured the leader described in that phrase as someone *in front of* an audience and standing on a stage behind a pulpit speaking truth. Resist. Think instead of someone further along the path, or someone who goes first. We want leaders who *lead*—in other words they *go* before us. Unfortunately, we typically think a leader who leads is one who gets things done and is above us making decisions. That is the world's way, but not the Kingdom's.

This assumption of vertical leadership creates a hierarchical institution so pervasive that even the translators of the New Testament cannot help but impose that view on the Scriptures. The translators of most English New Testaments insert the word "office" when talking about elders in 1 Timothy 3:1. The word "office" is not in the Greek text, but supplied by the translators because they cannot see a leader any other way. Hebrews 13:7 commands us in many versions to "Remember those who rule over you, who have spoken the word of God to you." But the actual words (ἡγουμένων ὑμῶν) are not "rule over" but "stand before"—or literally, "go first." Think of a journey, not a meeting hall, and the leader is a guide that goes ahead.[1] A movement is a journey and is found on a path. A leader is someone who goes first, not who "rules over" others. In a movement, every leader is a learner, and every learner can be a leader of someone. The question is not who is above and who

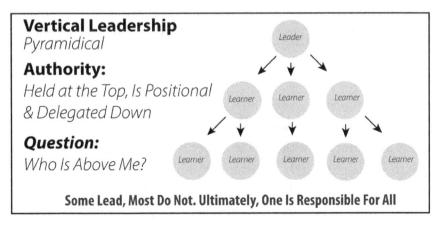

Figure 10.1

is below, but rather who is further down the path and can help us find our way forward. This is movemental rather than institutional.

We must allow our minds to reimagine leadership. It is not as though the Scriptures are unclear. Jesus emphasized over and over again that the first are last and the greatest are the least. Good and bad leadership are placed in contrast with very clear prepositions that illustrate the difference between the two (Matthew 20:24-26; Mark 10:41-43; 1 Peter 5:1-3). Bad leaders tend to be found "over" the people, and good leadership is found "among" them.

In a lateral leadership model, every person is on the path to Christ-likeness. There are always some that can follow in your footsteps, and there are always others further along that can help you find your footing on the path ahead. There is no organizational ladder to climb, and no one is above another.

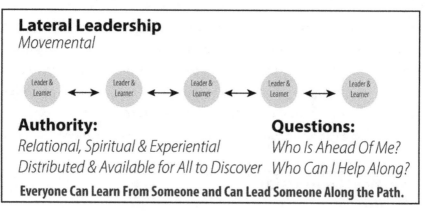

Figure 10.2

A pyramid can be a beautiful and long-lasting structure, but it doesn't move. The Kingdom of God is meant to be a movement.

A huge problem with vertical authority structure is the assumption that those above us in the structure are inherently better than we are—more together, more gifted, more knowledgeable, more experienced. Truthfully, those higher in the pyramid have just as many flaws and insecurities. In fact, they have more to live up to and more to lose.

As a result of this skewed view of leadership, we believe we are all accountable to those above us who are better than us and can be responsible for us. The truth is that those below have just as much spiritual endowment from Jesus as those above. You simply cannot have a movement if the people do not feel empowered to carry it forward.

We are so accustomed to vertical leadership that we cannot imagine real accountability without someone above taking responsibility for those beneath them. We even create a language to substantiate this view. We call leadership a "covering." We ask of others, "Who is your covering?" This implies that someone is over them to protect them and sanction their activity.

Actually, there can be far greater accountability if it is lateral rather than vertical. The New Testament consistently puts the responsibility for the local church's accountability on "one another." There are fifty-nine "one another" commands in the New Testament, many repeated. When you read them, it is remarkable how many of the functions we typically reserve for leaders are to be accomplished by all of us together (laterally). Here are some examples. We are to teach and admonish one another (Romans 15:14; Colossians 3:16). We are to carry one another's burdens (Galatians 6:2). We are to confess to one another (James 5:16). We are to encourage and build up one another (1 Thessalonians 5:11; Hebrews 10:24-25). We are to submit to one another (Ephesians 5:21). We are to serve others (minister) with our gifts (1 Peter 4:10). Leaders are always in the context of being "among," not "over."

7. Decentralized

In the West, most of what the Church has done for centuries has been cemented to physical buildings. As believers, we now want to see the kind of thing that happened in the book of Acts, but we do the kind of things that can never accomplish that. If everyone in a region had to attend one service on Sunday morning at the same location, do you think the gospel would have spread across the Roman Empire in one lifetime? Of course not.

An operating system (OS) that can work in a decentralized environment can also work in a centralized one, but it will not work the other way around. An OS that is centralized will not bust loose and suddenly work in a decentralized manner. So if we want rapid multiplication movements, we would be wise to steer clear of systems that are dependent upon or conducive to centralized environments.[2]

8. Obedience-oriented

For far too long, we have allowed a form of learning that requires little or no action in response. In fact, it seems we reinforce disobedience every single week just in the way we conduct our church services. People hear a new sermon every week, with little accountability to obey what they have heard the week before.

Can you do the math and determine how many sermons you have heard in your life? Probably not. I would guess that there are very few sermons you can even remember. I suggest that we can do this better. Discipleship should be obedience-oriented. I recommend that we don't teach a second lesson until the concepts of the first one are obeyed. I also would add that a lesson isn't truly understood until it is passed on to others. We all know that we learn more by teaching than we ever could by just hearing someone teach.

Part of our problem is we have invested so much in teaching, without requiring response or action, that we now evaluate maturity based upon retained knowledge. The level of education is now our determinant for leadership. The more we know, the greater our potential to be seen as a leader. That is as foolish as it is prevalent.

Every week is another chance for our senior pastors to show us what they know. Most church members become recipients of information but not agents of transformation. What if we never gave another sermon until the first sermon was actually practiced? Would that slow down the work or speed it up? I would argue that we would accelerate movements if we did so.

9. Use of filters

A study of discipleship movements throughout history demonstrates a consistent factor: filtering. What is filtering? It is where disciples are determined based upon obedience, and we invest in those who give visible evidence they are growing in the faith. That's not to say that everyone has their act together—in fact, quite the opposite is true. In rapid movements, everyone carries some baggage that takes years to shed. Multiplication movements are messy and chaotic, but they are also alive and expanding. The issue is not perfection but progression. Progression in obedience to the voice of the Shepherd is what we are looking for. When you find it, everything else becomes easier—much easier.

Jesus told the parable of the four soils (Mark 4:1-20) and then explained that if we miss this parable, all the understanding of the Kingdom is lost. It is the start of everything in the Kingdom.

In the parable, three of the four kinds of soil receive the message and sprout up quickly—but only the good soil bears fruit. If we impose a percentage on this (which is hypothetical), we would say only 33 percent of the people who accept our message will bear fruit, and that could be discouraging. For me it is not discouraging but life affirming. This parable has set me free in every sense of the word. Why?

For years, I experienced the reality of this parable in how people responded to me when I shared the gospel with them. When two-thirds of the new converts "fell away," I assumed I was doing something wrong. As a responsible leader, I felt it must be my fault. But it wasn't—Jesus said in advance that it would be this way. Yet we have forgotten this foundational parable and end up taking responsibility for others' obedience. As a result, we often adjust our churches to accommodate people who are not good soil. We don't ask much from them, and we invest heavily in making them as comfortable, entertained, and happy as can be, for fear we will lose some of our bad soil to the church down the street.

We have all been trained to think that the entire church must act in unison, and we must not leave anyone behind. Often, however, the bad soil in a church is reluctant to change or move forward in any direction, and end up carrying a type of veto power. Bad soil doesn't want to take responsibility; in fact, it wants others to take responsibility for it. As a result, the church does not move forward into any positive change but continues to babysit bad soil. We give our entire church experience to gathering and entertaining bad soil.

While bad soil doesn't bear fruit, it does tend to be more vocal. Most churches are actually dominated by the needs of bad soil, and the good soil spends all its time trying to please the bad. In such an instance, even the good soil in our churches has its fruit stunted by the distractions of the bad.

For most churches, we actually define success by the total amount of soil we attract rather than any fruitfulness coming from the soil. The churches that accumulate the most soil are the "best" churches. The results? Very little fruitfulness.

The solution is to filter out the unfruitful soil of unresponsive people early in the process of disciple making and leadership formation. That is why filtering is so prevalent when movements are actually happening.

I am not suggesting that we kick people out. Nor am I suggesting that we reduce the scope of those we share the message with. I am suggesting that we focus our energy and resources on the good soil. We cannot discern the good soil from the bad without first planting the seed. It is those who obey the Lord's voice that we want to empower, not those who complain the loudest. The sower in the parable sows the seed abundantly all over the place. Good soil is recognized by how it responds to the seed and what grows from it.

But what are we to do with the folks who are bad soil? Love them. We are commanded to love one another. We are commanded to love our neighbors. We are even to love our enemies, so I'm pretty sure love is the right answer for bad soil. But true love doesn't enable the poor choices of bad soil. So filtering is key, for both the good soil and the bad.

If we think that spending more time singing praise songs, listening to sermons, and asking them to give a bit of their money once a week will transform bad soil into good soil, we are deluded. Bad soil can become good soil but not by our efforts. Only God can do that. How does bad soil become good? It is turned upside down, death and waste are pressed into it, and it is left in isolation to remain fallow for a time. Hearing a devastating diagnosis from a doctor can turn soil inside out overnight. Getting a pink slip at work. Losing a loved one. Getting caught and exposed in our darkest secrets can transform someone from bad soil to good. That is God's work. We can pray, but our programs and preaching will not cause that transformation.

So at the grassroots of movement, we must *filter*. Love everyone, but pour our lives into the good soil. All ten lepers were healed (Luke 17:11-19); only one became a fruit-bearing follower. Jesus really loved the rich young ruler (Mark 10:17-22), but at the same time He filtered him out with harsh words. Was that the loving thing to do? Yes. Pride and greed were keeping this man from following Jesus, so Jesus brought his attention to the Law, which humbles us all and shuts our mouths. The Law reveals that we need a savior, so the rich young ruler needed the Law at that moment. Jesus was loving him and filtering him at the same time.

We will almost always be surprised about what happens when we let obedience filter the soil. Those with perceived potential who we think will change the world will let us down. Those we believe have little to no potential will rise up to great fruitfulness.

The predominant form of filtering in historical movements is accomplished simply by persecution. Bad soil, according to Jesus, cannot endure the heat of persecution. A church that has the bad soil filtered out of it is very fruitful—multiplying thirty times, sixty times, and a hundred times. But I do not believe we have to wait for persecution to start filtering—all we have to do is look for obedience and invest in it, and stop letting the loud, bad soil dictate all rules of engagement.

Whatever we celebrate tends to get our attention and pursuit. We need to change our culture and celebrate the right things. Shifting our view of what kind of success is worthy of celebration is key. Rather than celebrating the abundance of bad soil we have accumulated, we should celebrate those who are obedient to the voice of the Shepherd. That alone can change everything.

10. Culturally transferable and globally applicable methods

Filtering people who are serious about following Jesus from those who are not, is essential. But there is another type of filtering also needed. We must filter our methods and only hold to ones that multiply beyond our boundaries.

Back in the late 1990s, before there was such a thing as an organic church movement, a few of us had the dream of one. We were a handful of people committed to doing things in such a way that a multiplication movement would be birthed. We were so committed to multiplication that we put that big and awkward word in our name and called ourselves Church Multiplication Associates. Our level of commitment to multiplying became a litmus test of all we did—and still do. If we found a method that added to a church dramatically but never multiplied to the fourth generation, we would shelve it and move on. Everything was scrutinized by our value of multiplying. All our systems and methods had to meet the requirements of the qualities discussed in this chapter.

Early in those days, we set a goal for ourselves: that we would train people to plant churches all over the world. While it may be true that we are arrogant Americans who believe we have the answer for everyone's woes— that was not the reason for the goal. We set this goal simply because the Great Commission is to go to all the nations. We take Jesus' command both literally and seriously. If what we do in California doesn't work in Calcutta, it will not fulfill the Great Commission. So we would only promote what would work not just in the US but also in other cultures and languages.

These simple ideas changed everything. What would happen if all of us in church work scrutinized our methods in this way? Success would have a different metric. Large numbers and growth by addition would no longer be valued as success. Instead, empowerment of the many and reproduction to the fourth generation and beyond would be the level of success we strive for. Growth would go lateral rather than vertical.

Ministry methodology would simplify and empower all different people. Our work would become global and not remain merely regional.

We would not sacrifice the local for the global but rather see better influence in both. The scrutiny of extreme examination, to ensure these essentials are considered, eliminates a lot of stuff that would dilute the effects of the methodology.

Alternate ways to accomplish what is necessary

My good friend Alan Hirsch often says, "Our current systems are perfectly designed to see the results we are currently achieving." If we want different results, we will need new systems. There is no reason to ignore the needs that those systems are built to meet, but we simply must ask, "Is there a better way to meet those needs?"

If theological thinking is important, and higher academic institutions are stifling multiplication, let's ask if there is a better way. If biblical illiteracy is a problem and current discipleship methods are not providing a remedy, let's look for a better solution, rather than ignoring the need. When we elevate the method used to meet a need to a level as essential as the need itself, we create sacred cows that hinder all advancement. I know that we can do better. But to do so, we will have to be willing to let go of systems that prevent movement.

Below I will give you three examples of systems that are scalable, simple, and significant at the same time. Each of these examples—which cover evangelism, disciple making and theological education—are proven to be effective, with well over a decade of fruitfulness all over the world. All three share the characteristics outlined in this chapter and will help you see what a new OS can look like.

You can find these resources and more at our website: CMAResources.org.

Evangelism: The Seven Signs of John

In order to unveil the true Christ to any person open to seeing Him, we needed a means that was simple enough that everyone could do it in any culture, class, language, or age range. We also wanted the Scriptures to speak for themselves without needing a middleman to interpret them. That is a tall order to fill. We found our answer in the Bible—specifically, in the Gospel of John.

The *Seven Signs of John* is an evangelism method based on the words that the apostle John writes near the end of his gospel.

> *Therefore many other signs Jesus also performed in the presence of the disciples, which are not written in this book; but these have been written so that you may believe that Jesus is the Christ, the Son of God; and that believing you may have life in His name.*
> JOHN 20:30-31

Even though John was with Jesus from the start and saw all the miracles performed, he selected these particular miracles and included them in this specific order for a purpose—to open the eyes of the unbeliever to have faith in Jesus Christ and receive eternal life.[3] This is not my opinion; this is what the Scriptures themselves say. Consider it this way: the Holy Spirit is telling us that the miracle stories in the Gospel of John are the stories that are best to present Jesus Christ to an unbelieving heart. It is quite common for American Christian leaders to exaggerate the effectiveness of a method, but in this case it is the Holy Spirit making the claim, not me.

Here are the seven signs:

1. *The turning of water into wine (John 2:1-12)*
2. *The healing of the royal official's son (John 4:46-54)*
3. *The healing of the paralytic at the pool of Bethesda (John 5:1-17)*
4. *The feeding of the five thousand (John 6:1-14)*
5. *Jesus walking on water (John 6:15-25)*
6. *The healing of the man born blind (John 9:1-41)*
7. *The raising of Lazarus from the dead (John 11:1-46)*

Each week, we look at a different sign and encourage those we are sharing with to read the assigned story once every day. So every day of the first week, they read the story of Jesus turning water into wine. At the end of the week, when we meet and read the passage again together, we ask four simple questions and have a discussion about the passage. The questions are:

1. *What does this story say to you about people?*
2. *What does this story say to you about Jesus?*
3. *What does this story have to say about yourself?*
4. *Who needs to hear this story?*

This can easily be done by meeting once a week over a cup of coffee with anyone who is a spiritual seeker.

While this method is quite effective one-on-one, I believe its real brilliance is found in discussion within a small group. In every organic church I have ever started, we began by going weekly through these stories and simply asking the questions. I have yet to do this and not have someone commit to follow Christ and be baptized. I am not guaranteeing you the same results, but we can take the Holy Spirit's word for it that these stories will help people believe in Jesus.

This simple and profound ministry tool crosses all cultural barriers because it is simply the Bible speaking for itself. It is reproducible because anyone can ask the few easily remembered questions. This is not a model of church or a human curriculum. It is simply unleashing the power of God's Word to do what it does in an individual's life. To say that this doesn't work cross-culturally is to say that the Bible doesn't work cross-culturally. Even in an oral culture that is not literate, this tool will still work because it is basic storytelling.

At the end of the seventh sign (the raising of Lazarus from the dead), John mentions that many believed because of the miracle, but some didn't. This is a natural opportunity, presented by the Holy Spirit, to find out if the people hearing the stories will be those who believe in Jesus or not. Some respond, some don't.

This simple and highly transferable method can spread laterally, and it empowers anyone to plant the good seed in the soil. What comes next is a way to filter that soil so that the good soil is allowed to bear fruit—much fruit.

Disciple Making: Life Transformation Groups

The mission of the Church is not just to convert the lost but to make them disciples of Jesus. Ultimately, every church is only as good as her disciples. We need a disciple-making tool that has a simple pattern and can easily reproduce disciples—life-on-life.

A Life Transformation Group (LTG) is one reproducible pattern that allows every disciple to do two things: make other disciples almost immediately and connect each disciple to the Master Himself. These groups are potent catalysts for apostolic movements.

An LTG is made up of two to three people, all of the same gender, who meet weekly for personal accountability in the areas of their spiritual growth and development. A group should not grow beyond three but multiply into two groups of two rather than a single group of four.

There is no curriculum or training necessary for the LTG. The Bible and a simple bookmark that stays in the participant's Bible are all that are needed. A smartphone app is also available in English.[4]

The LTG consists of three essential disciplines for personal spiritual growth: confession of sin, a steady diet of repetitive reading of the Scripture, and prayer for others who need Christ.

The pattern is simple. Two or three people meet together. They have a card with character conversation questions on it; anyone can read them, but all answer. They also choose a book of the Bible they will read on their own the following week. They try to read twenty to thirty chapters in the week. If someone doesn't finish that much, they each read the same book again for the same amount. They continue this until all three finish the reading in the same week; then they move to another book. Some people think it is a lot of reading, but the idea is NOT to finish each week. The amount of chapters read is supposed to be a stretch so that it takes a few weeks to finish. If everyone finishes the thirty chapters every week, I suggest you beef it up to fifty chapters. The goal is not ticking off boxes but repetitive reading of whole books of the Bible in full context. This type of reading produces a much more thorough learning of Scripture than simply reading every book once in a year.

Each person in the group identifies three people that they want to see come to Christ, and they all write those names on their LTG cards. Every day they each take one of the names and pray for them.

The Life Transformation Group is a great filter for a movement. When someone comes to Christ, I immediately begin an LTG with him. From the first breath as a new creation in Christ, the disciple is taking in large volumes of Scripture in context, confessing his sins to others, and praying daily for the salvation of his friends (while he is still in close relational proximity).

Whenever someone is in trouble and needs counsel, my first suggestion is an LTG. If they object and say they only want counseling, I reply, "If reading Scripture, confession, and prayer doesn't help you, I guarantee my counsel will not be enough." I understand that there could be more issues of healing to deal with, but even that is accelerated when the person is daily reading Scripture, confessing in the context of safe relationships, and praying.

If someone is *not* interested in an LTG, I will usually decline counseling or mentoring him. This is my filter. That doesn't mean I don't care or that I am excluding these people from church. I am just granting them the choice of pursuing Christ in an LTG or not, and I am respecting their choice. This is my version of high-bar discipleship. I will mentor someone who is faithful in LTG but not if they find reasons to not do so. Obedience is the key that opens the door to opportunity. There's no judgment, just filtering.

An LTG does not require a leader in the group to decide things and provide expertise. There isn't a Bible study—just everyone hearing from God in the same book of the Bible. Self-guided discovery is the objective, and no one is the expert—all are learners. All those involved are experiencing the benefit of the group. I am not in an LTG to make a disciple but to be one. I don't need a second meeting or program on top of my discipleship group to enrich me as a leader of the group, because I am not the leader. The accountability isn't toward someone above or below me in a hierarchy but lateral. All of us are accountable to one another. I find that to be very similar to the way the New Testament describes church life.

This very simple method provides what is significant in transforming a life. The LTG does not change a life. The Holy Spirit, speaking through the Scripture to a heart prepared for it through honest and vulnerable confession, changes a life. The LTG is simply one way of bringing the elements of life change together into a system that all can do and that can transfer to other cultures and languages around the world. And it has.[5] My book, *Cultivating a Life for God: Multiplying Disciples through Life Transformation Groups*, is available for a limited time for free as an e-book on our website.[6] LTG Cards are also available at our website: www.CMAResources.org.

Theological Education: TruthQuest

TruthQuest is a revolutionary approach to training emerging leaders for church leadership. TruthQuest is not a workbook to study theology. Rather, TruthQuest is a community-based theological discovery system designed to equip leaders to continue the journey of lifelong learning. More than that, it is intended to help them introduce this lifelong journey to others who can, in turn, do the same. TruthQuest does not teach people *what* to think, but *how* to think—and that skill will serve them the rest of their lives.

It is hard to find something that not only teaches others but also can easily reproduce and multiply into the lives of succeeding generations. This is especially true when the subject is systematic theology. TruthQuest is designed to do just that. As its name implies, it is the beginning of a quest for truth—and this adventure will last a lifetime. TruthQuest is designed to equip emerging leaders to learn theology in a way that is practical, personal, and transferable into the lives of others. This sounds like an oversell that couldn't possibly be true. But when I explain how it is done, you will see how simple and yet profound it can be at the same time.

The learners are brought together into a monthly gathering of no more than eight and no less than four people to study theology together. The gathering will be on an agreed upon Saturday or Sunday of each month and will last approximately eight hours with a couple of breaks. These meetings can be scheduled for a complete year, minus a break for August and December. One all-day meeting each month is something that even those with a full-time job can do if they are motivated.

Theological education in TruthQuest is approached with what is termed an "incarnational" model of learning. Truth must be "fleshed out" in real-life experience, or the educational process has failed. In TruthQuest, all theology is examined through a grid of questions for life application.

Prior to the gathering, each learner will have studied the four points of a particular doctrine selected to be the focus of that month. The learners will utilize the Scriptures as well as two textbooks from two different theological points of view (all from an evangelical tradition— i.e. reformed, dispensational, Wesleyan, and charismatic) to study the doctrine.[7]

Each learner is to complete all the explanations for the doctrine and come to the gathering prepared to share his/her answers, as well as examples that illustrate the truth in real life. In other words, each learner comes prepared to teach the whole class all the four points of the doctrine but will be called upon randomly to teach a particular one. A timer can be used to set a limit to the length of time each learner will have to share his/her lesson. After the learner has finished the lesson, the facilitator will open up a discussion with the rest of the gathering by first asking if the presenter missed any important facet of the doctrine and then if the others would like to challenge the presenter's ideas. Again, a timer can be used to keep this discussion on task. Finally, if something goes unsaid or if an unsound theology emerges in the discussion, the facilitator may at that point interject his/her own point of view. Prior to this, he/she will only lead by asking questions of the participants.

Some "Brain Bruiser Discussion Questions" are included in each section of the Facilitator Guide[8] to help stimulate discussion if the learners themselves seem to have stalled. Answers, however, are not supplied. These questions are to generate discussion.

The journey to maturity is not traveled alone. Solomon, the wisest king in history said, "As iron sharpens iron, so one person sharpens another."[9] In a "round-table" format, the truth of God's Word is tested and internalized through the process of presenting thoughts, discussing, probing, and even debating with a team of peers. This Socratic approach instills a deeper level of learning because it is not merely memorizing facts for a test; it is holding the learned principles up in the crucible of debate and mutual experience. Self-directed learning is the objective, but in the light and scrutiny of interaction with other learners (peer mentoring).

We have found that those who go through the TruthQuest process performed better under the theological examination process of denominations than those who spent four years and $60,000 in a theological seminary. They not only know what they have chosen to believe, but they know why—and can explain their choice. They can also explain how the theology relates to their daily lives. This experience costs nothing more than the price of a couple of books and one Saturday a month for nine months.

Once someone has been through a year with TruthQuest, they are already equipped to lead another four to eight people through the same process the following year. Expertise is found in the textbooks and self-directed learning among peers.

If you would like to sample TruthQuest, it is best to acquire the Facilitator Guide first. You can get one here: www.cmaresources.org/truthquest-facilitators-guide.

Putting it all together

In our pursuit of multiplication movements, we invested much time, energy, money, and devotion in creating and evaluating systems that ultimately would not multiply and would not cross to other cultures and languages. It was hard to do, but we would shelve those resources, even when they were highly effective in growing a church in our own context. We refused to accept things that would not multiply and spread globally. There are probably three times as many resources on our shelves that don't meet our particular standards as there are those that do. But the few resources that we use, we use everyday and to the ends of the earth.

There are three criteria we use to evaluate every ministry system or method. We ask if each system can be:

1. **Received personally**. If a tool or system doesn't make a difference to us personally, we will not pass it on to others. This personal impact is essential. This is the stickiness factor. A changed life is the energy behind all movements. The system must bring together the biblical elements that change a life.

2. **Repeated easily**. If we can't communicate it in less than five minutes using only a sketch on a small napkin, then we are not likely to share it with others. Ministry in a multiplication movement is easy. We could explain all our methods in one sitting, and it would only take about fifteen to twenty minutes.

3. **Reproduced strategically**. This is the test of universal application. If the principles and methods can't be used in other cultures and languages, they are not going to fulfill the Great Commission. The first two methods mentioned above—the Seven Signs of John and Life Transformation Groups—pass this test. TruthQuest is limited in its scope to a literate culture with theological books available in that language. This limitation still allows for a few billion people to use it successfully, so we feel it is worthy of recommending and using, but alone it is insufficient to fulfill the Great Commission.

Going global

I sat at a long table in a strange land. Each person introduced himself to me. There were church planting leaders from multitudes of tribes throughout the Horn of Africa who told their stories. The photos of five other men were on the wall. These were the men who had given up their lives while serving Jesus that year. Others could show the scars of where they had been stabbed or shot in order to share the gospel. Many of the tribes represented would normally be at war with one another, but here they were worshipping and laughing together. So much joy was in the room. I felt both privileged and humbled to be there.

I took stock of the moment and had two thoughts at once. First, I realized that this moment was the fulfillment of a goal our small team at Church Multiplication Associates had set years earlier. I was about to teach people from a distant land how to start and multiply organic churches. The second thought was, "I have nothing to tell them. I should be listening to them, not the other way around. These are the real heroes, and I just want to hear from them." But I was about to be introduced, and I knew I would have to say something useful.

I glanced over at a long white wall with bold red letters written on it. It was their mission statement: *To fulfill the Great Commission in this generation in the Horn of Africa.* At that moment, I knew I had something important to tell them.

When my turn came to speak, I stood and humbly thanked them for the opportunity and confessed that I wasn't sure what I would say—until I saw their mission statement. I pointed at the wall, and all heads turned to see it.

I said, "I love you guys and love being here and hearing your stories— but I don't like your mission statement." All their heads immediately dropped in shame and embarrassment. I didn't want them to stay that way, so I explained, "Your vision is impossible to accomplish. You cannot fulfill the Great Commission in only the Horn of Africa. The Great Commission must go to 'all the nations.' It cannot be confined to your generation either; it is to go 'to the end of the age.'" And then to encourage them, I went a step further and explained, "We need your influence all the way to Los Angeles, California." Heads raised, and the beautiful smiles returned.

There is a saying in the environmental movement: *Think globally, act locally.* I believe that should be our own approach to ministry as well—to think about the global impact of our choices while making every effort to improve things right where we are. The Great Commission demands that.

Many years ago I traveled to Turkey to speak at a conference for Christian workers deployed all over Central Asia. Because it was a family conference, my two daughters were with me. We were also given the opportunity to enjoy a tour of the seven churches of Asia Minor mentioned in the book of Revelation.

After the conference wrapped up, we started to board the tour bus. A participant who had taken the earlier tour pulled me aside and said, "The tour guide, Emir, is a moderate Muslim, but open to the gospel." He had been given a Bible and had already been reading it. The participant asked me to pray and look for an opportunity to share the gospel with Emir.

On the first day, Emir and I sat at a café table slurping Turkish coffee. We are from very different worlds, so at first we smiled and slurped our coffee in uncomfortable silence. Finally Emir spoke up and said he had been reading the Bible lately. I smiled and said, "That's great." After another slurp I asked, "What is something you have learned from your reading?"

He thought about it and then said, "Well, I really love Jesus."

I put my cup down. I leaned forward toward him and looked directly into his eyes. He tensed up and even started to pull away just a bit. I said, "Jesus really loves you." Both of us felt goose bumps in that moment. While that was the extent of our conversation, it did leave a lasting impression.

At the final dinner of the tour, a group of missionary workers from tough places in Central Asia came up to my table and surrounded me. They said they had been talking and then announced, "We have a question for you." I smiled and welcomed them, saying, "Have at it. I don't promise I have all the answers, but I am open to any questions."

Chad, who worked in Kazakhstan, said, "Every other year we have pastors from the States come and teach us at this conference. They tell us what they do, share moving stories about incredible success, and get us all excited. Then we go home and try to do what they taught, and it never works in our context." He paused, looked at the faces of the others, then back at me, and asked, "What makes you any different?"

"That is a great question," I said. Because of our history of scrutinizing resources with a global perspective, I not only had an answer but I could explain why our ministry methods are different and do work in other cultures and contexts. So I replied, telling them much of what I have included in this chapter.

Afterward, I decided to give them an example. I grabbed a napkin from the table and listed the seven references from John's gospel and the four questions. I explained how it worked and asked, "Do you think that will work in your Muslim context?"

As he looked down at the napkin, a smile appeared on Chad's face. He looked up at me and said, "Yes, that may actually work." He got up and left the table, and the others joined him.

Chad left the dining hall after dinner, went downstairs to find Emir, and had him take out his new Bible and read John 2:1-11. A Muslim read a story about a prophet turning water into lots of wine for a party. Chad asked him the four questions—and Emir gave his life to Christ.

Chad then handed the napkin to Emir and told him to invite his friends and family to his home for dinner. "After dinner," he said, "read one of the stories and ask the same four questions."

Well, I would like to report that a rapid multiplication movement was ignited and spread across the Muslim world, but I never had any contact information to follow up. But it is possible. My point is that these simple and significant methods are transferable to other cultures and can empower ordinary people to pass on the extraordinary gospel.

A simple tool or method that allows the Scripture to speak for itself and that instigates self-directed learning can empower ordinary people to do some of the most important work we are called to do. Someone can accept Jesus in the morning and share Jesus in the afternoon. Such a method can go into all nations and be translated into all languages.

We can fulfill the Great Commission in our lifetime, but we will need to rethink how we go about doing it. There are better ways—if we are willing to let go of the old ones that have already proven that they will not work. To accomplish this, though, we would have to be a people worth multiplying, and that is what the next chapter addresses.

CHAPTER ELEVEN

Untouchable and Unshakeable: Being Someone Worth Multiplying

A man is rich in proportion to the number of things he can afford to let alone.
—Henry David Thoreau

I must be willing to give up what I am in order to become what I will be.
—Albert Einstein

LEGEND TELLS US A REMARKABLE STORY of the ancient Church Father John Chrysostom. He was an outspoken preacher who feared no man. He preached strongly against sin. Consequently, he offended church and government officials alike, including the unscrupulous Empress Eudoxia. Eventually, he was summoned before Emperor Arcadius himself. The encounter to determine Chrysostom's punishment proved to be more difficult for the emperor than could be imagined.

Emperor Arcadius first proclaimed that Chrysostom would be banished from the empire for his offense. The elderly man replied, "Sire, you cannot banish me, for all the world is my Father's house."

Taken aback, the emperor then responded, "Very well, then all your possessions will be confiscated."

Shaking his head, the preacher replied, "Sir, that also cannot be, for my treasure is in heaven, where moth and rust cannot destroy nor can thieves break in and steal."

As his desire to cause this man pain increased by the second, the emperor spit out, "Then I will drive you from man, to live and die in solitary confinement." For emphasis he added, "And you will have no friends left on earth."

The godly man simply said, "That you cannot do, either, for I have a Friend in heaven who has promised to never leave me nor forsake me."

Leaning back in exasperation with a wave of his hand, Arcadius finally said, "Then I will have you killed and be done with you."

The Church Father replied, "Then you will only do me a favor, for to live is Christ and to die is my gain. My true life is hidden with God in Christ and is not yours to give or take."

You can't hurt someone like this. This is what it means to be unshakeable.

Identity issues

What do you want people to notice about you? When you enter a place full of new acquaintances and you want to make a good impression, what are the traits you want them to notice first?

I have been in circumstances where I wanted to impress people, as I'm sure you have. At those times, I am amazed at what I put forward as my identity. I am an author of published books. I am a former athlete and lifeguard. I have traveled broadly. I have artistic skills. I associate with some famous people. I can be funny in front of a crowd. I am a church planter. I started a business. I am a homeowner. I am Dana's husband. I have three beautiful kids that have grown up to love and serve Jesus. My dad is a successful artist. My uncle is a legendary big wave surfing pioneer. I am a LA Lakers fan.

All of these things are true, but none of them are the best thing about me. These are not my identity—they are facts about me, but they are not who I am.

Have you ever tried to tell people who you are without telling them what you do, where you come from, what your family is like, or what things you prefer? It is not easy. Knowing our real identity—who we truly are—is harder than simply knowing what we do or where we are from. But truthfully, our identity is more important. Those of us who are new creatures in Christ are, unfortunately, not very in touch with our true identity. Like superheroes, we keep our true identity secret—we go through life hiding the person we really are, even from ourselves. A rather normal veneer outside covers a remarkable inside.

We all do this. Maybe you are the class clown and want to make everyone laugh. Perhaps you have always been the beauty queen or Miss Congeniality. Are you the nerd that others turn to for answers for the tests? Some are the jocks, and their bodies evidence their hard work. Perhaps you are an entrepreneurial go-getter and "success" is your bumper sticker. Do you drive a fancy car and wear the best in fashion? Are you a foody? A coffee snob? An urban hipster? An indie artist or popular DJ? Is social activism your outer shell? All of these things can be impressive in their own way, but none are permanent. None compare with Christ in you, the true hope of glory.

I encourage you to make a list of the seven things that are most important to you. Take your time. Pray over the list. Now make a list of the five qualities about yourself that you feel are most significant and unique. Pray over that as well.

Now, look over both lists and ask yourself this: *what could be taken from me by thieves, decay, sickness, or someone dying?* What is left behind? If anything is left on the list, *that* is the unshakeable you. Whatever is left is not only the unshakeable you, but is also likely the best part of you.

Christ in you is the hope of glory—and nothing else is.

Stripping away the veneer

Strip away the veneer. Reveal the real. Who you are when no one is looking is the true you. The real you must be the same even when everyone is looking. Who you are is truly more important than what you do.

We are all in a process to let the real us out. Life is designed to strip away all the overlaid identities and bring out the true you hidden inside—the you that has been redeemed by Jesus…*the new you.*

You mature by intentionally bringing to the surface the real, redeemed you. Maturity comes when you readily strip away the surface to allow the redeemed identity of Christ to emerge as your true self. You are mature when you see the value of the stripping process and begin to cooperate with it. Then you are prepared to help others do the same. To grow, you have to let the old person die away, including letting go of things that were once the most important parts. That can be painful and hard to do.

We cannot hold to one identity and still allow the other to come out. We have to choose. Either we hold to the old or we abandon it for the new. As John the Baptist proclaimed, "He must increase, but I must decrease" (John 3:30).

I believe persecution is a tool that strips our outer layers so that our inner being will reflect the beauty of Christ within—if indeed it is there to be discovered. Perhaps that is why the filtering of persecution always results in a purer and more powerful expression of God's Kingdom. It forcibly removes the things we tend to think are so important, to reveal the only truly significant things we have. It doesn't allow us to place value in lesser things such as external personalities, property, positions, and programs. Priorities are clarified. Choices are made simple. Realities become clear. Christ becomes all…or nothing.

Under the threat of persecution, we are forced to choose what is truly valuable and what is not. What do you truly live for? What would you die for?

The sooner we can get to this sense of identity, the better prepared for this age we will be. Anything less than this type of spiritual understanding will have devastating consequences in the very near future as this age crashes in on us like a tidal wave. We do not have to wait for persecution in order to walk in this reality. We can choose this way of life now. The sooner we do, the more at rest we will be as the world around us spins increasingly out of control. This is the secret to a future-proof faith. When we find ourselves content in Christ and unshaken by the chaos of this world, we will become a people worth multiplying.

Questions to ponder

Is the Spirit of Christ seen in you? Do others see within you Christ incarnate? Are you living in such a way that others see Christ in you and ask, "Where does that come from?" Are you willing to cooperate with the stripping away of the outer veneer of lesser identities so that Christ can shine more obviously?

1. *When will Christ be enough?*
2. *What will it take for Christ to be the most noticeable thing about you?*
3. *How can you cooperate with the Holy Spirit's stripping process? What do you need to let go of as your identifying characteristics so that Christ becomes your core identity?*

Stripping the lesser reveals the greater you

Every young man has a deeply felt internal need to have a father who will teach him how to be a man. This unconscious drive pushed me around for a few years, searching for a mentor who would love me and show me what being a man, a husband, and a father is really all about. My search ended when I married Dana and was accepted into her family.

My father-in-law, Ray Walker, was a real man. He was a cop for thirty years on the streets of Los Angeles. He worked as a detective in all sorts of neighborhoods. But he wasn't just a tough guy—he was a godly man who had a great sense of humor and loved everyone. His job was not his master, and being a cop was not his core identity. He would leave his work at the office. When he came home, he was a dad and a husband, not a cop. Wherever he was—at work on the streets of LA or at home with his family—he was an unashamed follower of Jesus.

Of course, at first it was intimidating to date a girl whose father carried a sidearm and could open my files and investigate all my records at any time. As I got to know Ray, however, he was anything but intimidating. He was very vulnerable and accessible as a person. I learned what the term "gentleman" meant by watching Ray. He was all man, yet always gentle.

Soon we became the closest of friends. He became the father I needed, and in a sense, I became the son he never had, though he had three beautiful daughters. We would tell each other everything and had no secrets between us.

Ray showed me how to be both manly and still be a gentle and loving dad. He showed me how to be a faithful husband. I learned how to take responsibility and lead in a quiet and humble manner from this man. We loved to be together; we would have fun no matter what we were doing. We were not just family; we were best friends.

Ray was best known for his generosity and friendly personality that could find a corny joke for any occasion. Too many times to count, he covered my financial needs in those early years of my marriage to Dana. No matter how hungry we would be while trying to support a family of five on several part-time jobs, we would always have a good meal when we were with Ray. For over a decade, I didn't have to buy a car because he would always give me his old car when he bought a new one—and he always took immaculate care of his cars.

A few years ago, Ray started forgetting things. Small things misplaced turned into big things forgotten. Eventually he was diagnosed with dementia, probably from early onset Alzheimer's disease. He even became confused about who his closest companions were.

Caring for someone like this is not easy. Dana and I took him into our home for periods of time to relieve June, his wife. This was both the hardest and easiest decision we ever had to make. Dana had to stop working, which set us back financially, but that was not a concern. We looked after him. I shaved him, bathed him, dressed him, and cleaned up after him. He was a constant companion. But this was not a burden. It is hard to explain, but I loved the man so much that this was not hard at all to do. I much preferred having him in this condition to being without him at all.

So many times I prayed for his healing. At one point he even seemed healed for a moment and then faded back into the grey cloud of the disease. I couldn't understand why God would allow such a good man to suffer such a horrible disease. I still do not have an answer, but I can say that I saw something beautiful that God showed us all in this ordeal.

It may sound strange, but watching this godly man live through this horrible disease actually raised my respect for him. It is common for some to say that the person who suffers from Alzheimer's loses their personality, and it's true they can sometimes become angry and hurtful people. That was not the case for Ray. He never stopped exhibiting the things I loved about him.

Whenever we were out and a waiter would present the check to pay, Ray would instinctively reach for his back pocket and say, "I've got this." Of course he hadn't had a wallet in a long time, but he still had his generosity. It was a great honor to buy his meals after all the times he bought mine.

When we were out and he would meet a new person, he always had a smile and a kind nod. He would search for a joke with a punch line that was no longer in his files, but I could tell he still had his sense of joy. We had all heard the joke so many times that it was easy to finish the joke for him.

The strangest thing for me was when Ray came with me to our organic church family. He couldn't remember people's names, but he knew the words to the songs and sang them as well as ever. When he prayed, his prayers were articulate and clear. Many times I would have to raise my head and open my eyes and see if that was really Ray praying. I realized that the disease could take his mind but not his soul or the Spirit of Christ in him.

Dementia strips away a person's sense of identity. All the stuff Ray used to know and the things he used to take for granted were violently ripped away. His mind was taken from him. His memories were stolen. But his soul, his true self, was not taken from him. Jesus remained with Ray from start to finish.

I stayed beside Ray until the very end. On his last night, I stayed by his bed, praying and thanking God for his life while he labored to breathe. His own body was forgetting how to work, as the disease spread through his mind voraciously.

Finally I put my hand on his arm one last time, turned to heaven, and said, "Lord, take my friend home." In that very moment, Ray released his last breath, and his soul left his body. I felt privileged to have been in the room when his mind went from a dark cloud of nothing to fully knowing "just as he is fully known" (1 Corinthians 13:12). I looked up and with tears running down my face, said out loud, "Bye, Ray, I love you. Thank you for everything. I will see you soon enough."

I saw so much godliness in Ray when we laughed together and walked through life together while his mind was as sharp as a tack. Alzheimer's is a horrible disease, but I saw Jesus in Ray even through that experience. I saw a man walk with God through the darkest night of the soul and emerge victorious. I only hope that I can live my life with the same joy, generosity, and dogged faith that Ray did. He was Christ incarnate for me, even in the midst of serious dementia. Ray's faith remained intact. His faith was unshaken by the greatest challenge one can face. I only hope that I can pass whatever test awaits me.

As we have learned throughout this book, the world is an increasingly chaotic place. Our security seems always in peril. But Christ is the same yesterday, today, and forever. His Kingdom is unshakeable. The gates of hell themselves cannot prevail against the people who find their sense of identity and purpose in Him.

Discover who you were always meant to be. Find your security in Him and you will be future-proof—and you will be someone worth multiplying.

The End of the Beginning

The world is a dangerous place to live, not because of the people who are evil,
but because of the people who don't do anything about it.
—Albert Einstein

Every new beginning comes from some other beginning's end.
—Seneca

ONE SUMMER DAY while I was guarding the beachgoers at Venice Beach, I almost met my end. Some moments are defining in life—they leave scars that we carry with us every day after. My youth ended on that day, and I began living with greater purpose because of an awareness of how fragile life is. From that time forward, I lived as if every day could be my last. Ironically, thinking about death has actually brought me more life.

The earth shook with the crashing of giant waves. The surf seemed to grow with each swell until the waves were licking the top of the twenty-foot high pier where my tower stood, but the sets were not coming in rapid succession. The lulls between sets of waves were deceptively calm and lured unsuspecting patrons into the water to cool off. The swimmers thought the strong northerly current was the only hazard they had to fight. As is often the case, they underestimated the incredible power of the Pacific. This was the kind of day when lifeguards earn their money.

One tourist was losing his fight to stay in front of his beach towel, drifting up closer to the pier. The horizon line should be constant, so he was shocked when it began to gobble up more of the blue sky. The giant swells seemed to consume the entire ocean view. He was too far out to make it to the beach but not far enough out to escape the breaking mammoths—stuck in the impact zone and accelerating toward the pier. He decided to go with the flow of the current and started swimming for the cement pilings, hoping they could protect him from the waves' crushing power. That is not how this works. We were about to find out what happens when an unstoppable force meets an immovable object— and a skinny European tourist gets in between.

Anticipating the disaster, I strapped my rescue can over my head and shoulder and raced to get to him before the waves did. He was clinging onto the barnacles, bracing himself for the impact. It was close, but I beat the waves—and they were not happy about it.

I pried his fingers off the razor-sharp barnacles that were much better suited to cling to the cement pillars than he was. As soon as he let go, the current took him out from under the shadow of the pier, and the giant waves simply knocked him, skinny Speedos and all, onto the sand where he was safe. I was a different story.

I watched him clear the pier just in time for the first wave to grab me and shoot me headfirst like a bullet toward a cement piling. Two thoughts flashed though my brain in that instant: "I have no control and am completely helpless," and "This is the last moment of my life."

My life didn't flash before my eyes. I didn't think about loved ones or regrets. I only had time to squeeze my eyelids shut and prepare to be smashed.

When I was only a couple feet and a fraction of a second from impact, a miracle happened that seemed to defy all the laws of physics. My body suddenly stopped moving, but the water continued to rush past me. What the...?!

My mind immediately accepted it as a miracle, but how did this happen? While I had been treading water and loosening the victim's grip, my "rescue can" wrapped around the piling next to him—and never has a device been more appropriately named. The slack of the towrope was just short enough to keep me from a cracked skull, broken neck, and inevitable appearance before the ultimate Judge of all.

Relief flooded my mind but immediately vanished when I realized I was still in the foam of crashing waves under the pier's shadow, surrounded by barnacle-covered pillars, and being held there—underwater. Air was beyond my reach, but death was within inches in every direction.

The very thing that initially appeared to save my life against the rising tidal force could actually become my death. Delay was not an option. I immediately unstrapped the rescue can and kicked for sunlight, praying that I wouldn't crash into an immoveable object on my way. Never had sunlight looked more delightful as the hazards of the shade passed behind me. I rode the next wave onto the sand, stood up, and walked onto the beach, shaken but completely unharmed. When I turned to look at the death trap I had miraculously escaped, my rescue can washed up beside my feet, as if to commiserate with me.

Mike Frazier, the lifeguard at the next tower, ran to me shouting, "Are you okay?" After I nodded, he added, "That was amazing!" He paused briefly to think about how to tell me his next thought. Finally he said bluntly, "I have to tell you—there is no way I was going in there to help you." His obvious intelligence is likely what propelled him to become the chief of LA County lifeguards—and I changed my vocation within a year but fondly remember all my summers at the beach.

The Church of Jesus Christ faces a situation similar to my harrowing experience. Lulled into a false sense of security, local churches are now in a situation with few good options. The rising water of tidal waves is rapidly pounding over our heads. We feel helpless as we are being tossed about like an insignificant rag doll. It is easy to believe the solution is to tie ourselves down to something stable and wait it out, but that would be our end. Staying tied to an anchor submerged under the rapidly rising water provides us no better escape from the crashing forces. We cannot stay where we are, or we will die. We must move forward with the current and find a way to ride this wave into the light and onto shore. That is our only viable choice.

Are we approaching the time of Jesus' return?

For tens of thousands of years, humankind has used light and shadows to tell stories on a wall. Using that ancient technology—by way of an overhead projector—I stood before my congregation with three lists of ingredients displayed on a screen behind me. I was the pastor of a normal church in a suburban neighborhood outside of Los Angeles at the time. It was the late 1990s, and we were still on a more forgiving slope of technological advancement, clueless about how all our lives would change in the coming decade.

"Before you," I said, "are three lists of the main ingredients in brands of candy you can find at any convenience store in the world. Can any of you tell me what the candies are just by reading the ingredients?"

People guessed—some were right, most were not.

Then I displayed the same lists but beside them were the names — Reese's Peanut Butter Cups, Snickers, and Peanut M&M's. Now these candies are all very different in size, shape, texture, and taste, but not so different in ingredients. I announced, "These are the types of candy, but they are not in the correct order. Can you connect the ingredients to the right name?"

Even with the names of the products, people couldn't easily match the correct ingredients to their product.

I asked, "If you saw only these lists of ingredients on a shelf in a convenience store, would they entice you to buy the product, sight unseen? Would they make you hungry? Would these printed words make your mouth water? Could you know what you are buying and how it would taste by just reading the list of ingredients?"

If I ask you the same questions, the obvious answers are "no." You can use certain parts of your brain to imagine what it would taste like, but only when it is in contact with your taste buds does your brain actually experience the taste.

The Bible tells us about the end of times when Jesus will return to earth, but all we have is a list of ingredients. People have theories about what the end will look like, feel like, and taste like, but I believe the final product will surprise us all.

Whether you are premillenial, postmillennial, amillenial, pre-trib, post-trib, mid-trib, or no-trib in your eschatology, I am confident of one thing: everyone is wrong about some aspect they believe about that time. What actually happens will be a surprise—*to everyone*. We cannot be certain of how things will happen based upon study of the Bible, just like we cannot know how a dish tastes simply by reading its recipe. Words on a paper do not melt in your mouth with sweet warmth and fill your senses with delight like taking a bite of the real thing. A list of ingredients just can't compare to the real thing.

That said, I believe we are closer in time to the events recorded in the book of Revelation than those of the book of Acts. I also believe, in these perilous times, we are very close to experiencing the types of stories found in the book of Acts.

When you look at the exponential increases discussed in the first section of this book, how can you not believe we are closer to the end than we are to the beginning? The expiration date on Planet Earth has to be close.[1] We may be at the beginning of the end. We are definitely at the end of the beginning. Let me explain what I mean by that.

Some call the long, slow rise of a chart showing the exponential curve "the long tail." Others call it the hockey stick. I like to call it the runway. If you take a plane from one end of a runway to the other end, you have not gone anywhere. The runway is not the journey; it is just the start, the launch. The long tail leading to the exponential growth curve is behind us. The slow build is over, and we are now rising quickly toward the end. We are flying now. The beginning is over. We can soar or crash, but we cannot go back.

Everything that has come before was to take us to this place in history. The prelude is done, and now we are heading quickly to the climax. There is no going back, the beginning is over, and the end is approaching rapidly.

These are the days when we will show the world our worth. We are close to seeing the reality of God's Kingdom on earth in tangible ways that none can deny. Given all that is happening in this world right now, we must be prepared.

This book is to raise our awareness of how significant it is that we change now or lose the fight. I wanted to alert the people of the Kingdom of God to how much ground we have already lost, spent on futile ambitions. But this book is not meant to instill fear or dread—quite the opposite. I want to inspire hope and faith as we step into a future that cannot harm us, a future that is ours to win. I have not only articulated the very real threat to our existence, but I have also provided simple, clear, and effective means to thrive. There are solutions. The Church will not be overcome, but the old ways must be.

When the water around you rises, staying tied to old forms of doing church can be deadly. Jesus is the anchor for our souls, not the old mechanisms of church. Unleash yourself from the strap that is holding you submerged to old ways that may have saved you in the past but can only suffocate you now. Swim for the light.

ACKNOWLEDGEMENTS

I wish to acknowledge the following:

Ralph Moore, Curtis Sergeant, Alan Hirsch and Carol Davis have all sharpened my thinking about missional movements.

Dezi Baker is my global partner in catalyzing movements. He and his team have shown us all what can be in this encroaching future. His prophetic balance to my apostolic role has made me a better person and our work more effective.

Tony and Felicity Dale have been friends and a constant support in times when no others have.

Tammy Dao and LoveHOP (our church) have been my gracious ministry home and willing guinea pigs for what is to come. My future is brighter because you are part of it.

Timothy Wong has graciously helped to get this book published and its message out.

Val Gresham, my editor, has helped me to communicate succinctly and well.

Anna Robinson has provided valuable assistance to the manuscript with her very capable proofreading and suggestions.

NOTES

CHAPTER 1: TOO MANY RATS IN THIS RACE

1   Upton Sinclair, *I, Candidate for Governor: And How I Got Licked* New Ed. edition (University of California Press, 1994), p. 109.

2   Max Roser and Esteban Ortiz-Ospina, "World Population Growth," 2013, updated April, 2017. https://ourworldindata.org/world-population-growth .

CHAPTER 2: THE SKYNET IS FALLING

1   Ray Kurzweil, "The Law of Accelerating Returns," March 7, 2001. http://www.kurzweilai.net/the-law-of-accelerating-returns .

2   "Big Idea: Technology Grows Exponentially," Big Think. http://bigthink.com/think-tank/big-idea-technology-grows-exponentially .

3   Claire Brownell, "Google Inc's AI guru Ray Kurzweil talks failure, nano-robots, and the singularity in Waterloo," *Financial Post*, May 12, 2016. http://business.financialpost.com/fp-tech-desk/google-incs-ai-guru-ray-kurzweil-talks-failure-nano-robots-and-the-singularity-in-waterloo?__lsa=6a62-3920 .

4   Jenn Gidman, "Computer manages to beat 4 of world's best poker players," Fox News, February 1, 2017. http://www.foxnews.com/tech/2017/02/01/computer-manages-to-beat-4-worlds-best-poker-players.html .

5   "Why has Google bought an AI company?" BBC News, January 28, 2014. http://www.bbc.com/news/technology-25927797 .

Evan Ackerman and Erico Guizzo, "Google Acquires Seven Robot Companies, Wants Big Role in Robotics," IEEE Spectrum, December 4, 2013. http://spectrum.ieee.org/automaton/robotics/industrial-robots/google-acquisition-seven-robotics-companies .

6   'Kevin Rawlinson, "Microsoft's Bill Gates insists AI is a threat," BBC News, January 29, 2015. http://www.bbc.com/news/31047780 .

7   Rory Cellan-Jones, "Stephen Hawking warns artificial intelligence could end mankind," BBC News, December 2, 2014. http://www.bbc.com/news/technology-30290540 .

8   Peter Holley, "Bill Gates on dangers of artificial intelligence: 'I don't understand why some people are not concerned,'" *The Washington Post*, January 29, 2015. https://www.washingtonpost.com/news/the-switch/wp/2015/01/28/bill-

gates-on-dangers-of-artificial-intelligence-dont-understand-why-some-people-are-not-concerned/?utm_term=.28edf35f526d .

9   Aatif Sulleyman, "AI Is Highly Likely to Destroy Humans, Elon Musk Warns" *The Independent*, November 24, 2017. https://www.independent.co.uk/life-style/gadgets-and-tech/news/elon-musk-artificial-intelligence-openai-neuralink-ai-warning-a8074821.html .

10   Neil Strauss, "Elon Musk The Architect of Tomorrow," *Rolling Stone*, November 15, 2017. http://www.rollingstone.com/culture/features/elon-musk-inventors-plans-for-outer-space-cars-finding-love-w511747 .

11   There are many who speculate that AI will not be a threat to humanity, but an enhancement. Diamandis and Kurzweil are strong advocates of the benefits of AI and Human integration. A good read that is very optimistic is Peter H. Diamandis and Steven Kotler, *Abundance: The Future Is Better Than You Think* (Free Press, 2014).

12   Vangie Beal, "Moore's Law," Webopedia. http://www.webopedia.com/TERM/M/Moores_Law.html .

13   Thomas L. Friedman, *Thank You for Being Late: An Optimist's Guide to Thriving in the Age of Accelerations* (Farrar, Straus and Giroux, Kindle Edition), pp. 36-37.

14   In an interview with Rachel Courtland, Gordon Moore stated, "We won't have the rate of progress that we've had over the last few decades. I think that's inevitable with any technology; it eventually saturates out. I guess I see Moore's law dying here in the next decade or so, but that's not surprising." Rachel Courtland, "Gordon Moore: The Man Whose Name Means Progress, The visionary engineer reflects on 50 years of Moore's Law," IEEE Spectrum, March 30, 2015. https://spectrum.ieee.org/computing/hardware/gordon-moore-the-man-whose-name-means-progress .

15   Cade Metz, "The Race to Build an AI Chip for Everything Just Got Real," *Wired*, April 24, 2017. https://www.wired.com/2017/04/race-make-ai-chips-everything-heating-fast/ .

16   From notes in "Rhetorical Theory and Communication" with Sharon Downey, CSULB, Fall 1983.

17   Attributed to Orwell by John H. Bunzel, president of San Jose State University, as reported in Phyllis Schlafly, *The Power of the Positive Woman* (Jove Books,1978), p. 151; but not found in Orwell's works or in reports contemporaneous with his life. Possibly a paraphrase of Orwell's description of the rationale behind Newspeak in 1984.

18   G. Pryor, "Why Manage Research data?" in G. Pryor (Ed.), *Managing Research Data* (Facet Publishing, 2012), pp. 1-16.

19   Alex mentioned this in a talk and subsequently tweeted it.

20   Friedman, *Thank You for Being Late*, p. 31.

21   As told to Thomas L. Friedman and recounted in his book, *Thank You For Being Late*.

22   Tom Goodwin, "The Battle is For The Customer Interface," TechCrunch, March 3, 2015. https://techcrunch.com/2015/03/03/in-the-age-of-disintermediation-the-battle-is-all-for-the-customer-interface/ .

23   Kevin Ganville "Facebook and Cambridge Analytica: What You Need to Know," *The New York Times*, March 19, 2018 https://www.nytimes.com/2018/03/19/technology/facebook-cambridge-analytica-explained.html .

24   "What is Big Data Analytics?," IBM Analytics. https://www-01.ibm.com/software/data/bigdata/what-is-big-data.html .

25   "Big Data, for better or worse: 90% of world's data generated over last two years," *Science Daily,* May 22, 2013. https://www.sciencedaily.com/releases/2013/05/130522085217.htm .

26   Jacob Kastenakes, "US Senate Votes to let internet providers share your web browsing history without permission," *The Verge*, March 23, 2017. http://www.theverge.com/2017/3/23/15026666/senate-broadband-privacy-rules-congressional-review-act-fcc-vote .

27   Neil Strauss, "Elon Musk The Architect of Tomorrow," *Rolling Stone*, November 15, 2017. http://www.rollingstone.com/culture/features/elon-musk-inventors-plans-for-outer-space-cars-finding-love-w511747 .

28   Barton Gellman and Laura Poitras, "U.S., British intelligence mining data from nine U.S. Internet companies in broad secret program," *The Washington Post*, June 7, 2013. https://www.washingtonpost.com/investigations/us-intelligence-mining-data-from-nine-us-internet-companies-in-broad-secret-program/2013/06/06/3a0c0da8-cebf-11e2-8845-d970ccb04497_story.html?tid=pm_pop&utm_term=.4232a76e74b8 .

29   Zoe Kleinman, "Is your smartphone listening to you?" BBC News, March 2, 2016. http://www.bbc.com/news/technology-35639549 .

30   Peter Taylor, "Edward Snowdon interview: 'Smartphones can be taken over,'" BBC News, October 5, 2015. http://www.bbc.com/news/uk-34444233 .

31   "ACLU: Docs reveal 'Exponential' Growth of Domestic Spying,"
Common Dreams, September 29, 2012. http://www.commondreams.org/
news/2012/09/29/aclu-docs-reveal-exponential-growth-domestic-spying .

32   Peter Finn and Ellen Nakashima, "Obama defends sweeping surveillance
efforts," *The Washington Post*, June 7, 2013. https://www.washingtonpost.com/
politics/obama-defends-sweeping-surveillance-efforts/2013/06/07/2002290a-
cf88-11e2-9f1a-1a7cdee20287_story.html?hpid=z1&tid=a_inl&utm_term=.
a635ca0e7839 .

33   This is not entirely true. Law enforcement in many cities have installed
a device called the Sting Ray which acts much like a cell tower, but it skims your
cell phone data and is used for a variety of law enforcement purposes. It does this
indiscriminately to any and all who happen to pass within its reach. After some
initial outcry demanding transparency, a few guidelines for usage were put in
place, but these demands have gone mostly unheeded. Those we hired to "watch
over us" are now doing that in increasingly invasive and quite literal ways and
without accountability. Who is watching the watchmen? This violation of the
public trust is largely met without any repercussions. See Jazmine Ulloa, "Quietly,
A Cop Tool Skims Info: Despite Calls for Transparency, Police Say Little About
Device that Intercepts Cellphone Data," *Los Angeles Times*, August 27, 2017.
https://www.pressreader.com/usa/los-angeles-times/20170827/281505046349237 .

34   Daniel J. Solve, "Five myths about privacy," *The Washington Post*,
June 13, 2003. https://www.washingtonpost.com/opinions/five-myths-about-
privacy/2013/06/13/098a5b5c-d370-11e2-b05f-3ea3f0e7bb5a_story.html?tid=a_
inl&utm_term=.00fa1feadda5 .

CHAPTER 3: STUCK IN THE (SHRINKING) MIDDLE WITH YOU

1   Emma Seery et al., "Even It Up: Time to End Extreme Inequality,"
Oxfam, p. 8. http://www.oxfamamerica.org/static/media/files/even-it-up-
inequality-oxfam.pdf .

2   "America's Shrinking Middle Class: A Close Look at Changes Within
Metropolitan Areas," Pew Research Center, May 11, 2016. 2016 . http://www.
pewsocialtrends.org/2016/05/11/americas-shrinking-middle-class-a-close-look-
at-changes-within-metropolitan-areas/ .

3   Janet Adamy, "America's Middle Class Is No Longer The Majority," *The
Wall Street Journal*, Dec 9, 2015. http://blogs.wsj.com/economics/2015/12/09/
americas-middle-class-is-no-longer-the-majority/ .

4   Erik Sherman, "America Is the Richest, and Most Unequal, Country," *Fortune*, September 30, 2015. http://fortune.com/2015/09/30/america-wealth-inequality/ .

5   Reuters, "The World's 8 Richest Men Are now as Wealthy as Half the World's Population," *Fortune*, January 16, 2017. http://fortune.com/2017/01/16/world-richest-men-income-equality/ .

6   Ibid.

7   Erik Sherman, "America Is the Richest, and Most Unequal, Country."

8   Emma Seery et al., "Even It Up: Time to End Extreme Inequality," p. 6.

9   Tracy Jan, "Here's how much you would need to afford rent in your state," *The Washington Post*, June 8, 2017. https://www.washingtonpost.com/news/wonk/wp/2017/06/08/heres-how-much-you-would-need-to-make-to-afford-housing-in-your-state/?utm_term=.9605aa91aad0 .

10   US Debt Clock. http://www.usdebtclock.org/ .

11   "Bailout Recipients," Pro Publica. https://projects.propublica.org/bailout/list .

12   "In fact, $7.7 trillion of the secret emergency lending was only disclosed to the public after Congress forced a one-time audit of the Federal Reserve in November of 2011. After the audit the public found out the bailout was in trillions not billions; and that there were no requirements attached to the bailout money – the banks could use it for any purpose." Mike Collins, "The Big Bank Bailout," *Forbes,* July 14, 2005. https://www.forbes.com/sites/mikecollins/2015/07/14/the-big-bank-bailout/#773a35652d83 .

13   John Boyd, "What is the net worth of your elected member of Congress?" Chron, January 10, 2014. http://www.chron.com/news/politics/texas/article/What-is-the-net-worth-of-your-elected-member-of-5131789.php .

CHAPTER 4: ALL THE DEMONS ARE ON THE OTHER SIDE

1   Alan I. Abramowitz and Kyle L. Saunders, "Is Polarization a Myth?" *The Journal of Politics*. 70(2): 542 (April 2008).

2   Ibid.

3   "Us vs. Them," Tableau Public. https://public.tableau.com/en-us/s/gallery/political-polarization-us .

4   Pew Research Center, "Political Polarization in the American Public Section 1: Growing Ideological Consistency," June 12, 2014. http://www.people-press.org/2014/06/12/section-1-growing-ideological-consistency/#interactive .

5   Pew Research Center, "Political Polarization in the American Public: How Increasing Ideological Uniformity and Partisan Antipathy Affect Politics, Compromise and Everyday Life." http://www.people-press.org/2014/06/12/political-polarization-in-the-american-public/ .

6   Anger and hatred also tend to arrest the attention of the amygdala, which explains why news that once strove to be objective now feels free to express its biased anger at opposing viewpoints. Have you noticed that "commentary" that once was brief and was usually later in a news broadcast has now moved front and center and the more "objective" reporting is now only a support? Prime time news hours are now headlined by "journalists" that are only giving commentary.

7   Marc Siegel, *False Alarm: The Truth About the Epidemic of Fear* (Wiley, 2005), p. 15; Diamandis and Kotler, *Abundance*, p. 310.

8   Cass R. Sunstein, Republic.com. (Princeton University Press, 2001) pp. 5-6.

9   Ibid. p. 9.

10   Amy Mitchell et al., "Political Polarization & Media Habits," Pew Research Center, October 21, 2014. http://www.journalism.org/2014/10/21/political-polarization-media-habits/ .

11   Eli Pariser, *The Filter Bubble: What the Internet is Hiding from You* (Penguin Books, 2012).

12   For a good explanation of how the echo chamber divides and what is necessary to bridge, watch this Ted X talk by Theo E. J. Wilson who had to assume a false digital identity in order to even hear some of the deeper arguments of the other side of his worldview and begin to have compassion for people who think differently. "A black man undercover in the alt-right," TEDxMileHigh. https://www.youtube.com/watch?v=FdHJw0veVNY .

13   Douglas Quan, "Frequent texting and rapid-fire social media use could lead to 'moral shallowness': study," *National Post*, March 2, 2016. http://news.nationalpost.com/news/canada/frequent-texting-and-rapid-fire-social-media-use-could-lead-to-moral-shallowness-study .

14   Ray Oldenburg, *The Great Good Place* (Marlowe & Company, 1991).

15   Logan Annisette & Kathryn Lafreniere, "Social media, texting, and personality: A test of the shallowing hypothesis," Personality and Individual Differences, February 2016.

16   Jessie Cruickshank, "Challenges and opportunities in considering the Internet as a 4th Space for ministry."

17   It is worth noting that most of our discipleship and teaching methods in church focus upon trying to change lives via the semantic memory system. This is not only futile in changing a life, but also fosters an uncaring and unloving expression of Christianity, which in my opinion is the insidious side of how we disciple today. I believe the kind of Christianity we see today is a reaping of centuries of simply discipling people's semantic memory absent of real experience and relationships.

18   Cruickshank, "Challenges and opportunities in considering the Internet as a 4th Space for ministry."

19   "How challenges change the way you think," *Science Daily*, November 9, 2017. https://www.sciencedaily.com/releases/2017/11/171109093309.htm .

20   Thomas B. Edsall, "Trump Says Jump. His Supporters Ask, How High?" *The New York Times*, September 14, 2017. https://mobile.nytimes.com/2017/09/14/opinion/trump-republicans.html?action=click&pgtype=Homepage&clickSource=story-heading&module=opinion-c-col-right-region&region=opinion-c-col-right-region&WT.nav=opinion-c-col-right-region&referer=https://t.co/c6FlHbziMi .

21   Robert P. Jones, "Trump Can't Reverse the Decline of White Christian America," *The Atlantic*, July 4, 2017. https://www.theatlantic.com/politics/archive/2017/07/robert-jones-white-christian-america/532587/ .

CHAPTER 5: WE CAN NO LONGER AFFORD TO STAY WHERE WE ARE

1   He commanded us to make disciples by teaching them to obey his commandments, one of which is to make disciples by teaching them to obey his commands. Inherent in the Great Commission is multiplication.

2   Alina Tugend, "Donations to Religious Institutions Fall as Values Change," *The New York Times*, November 3, 2016. https://www.nytimes.com/2016/11/06/giving/donations-to-religious-institutions-fall-as-values-change.html .

3   Michael Frost, Alan Hirsch, *The Shaping of Things to Come: Innovation And Mission For The 21st Century*, Peabody, MA, Hendrickson Publishers, 2003, pp. 18-19, 225.

CHAPTER 6: VULNERABILITIES OF THE CHURCH

1   William A. Beckham, *The Second Reformation* (TOUCH Outreach Ministries, 1995), chapter two.

2   You can discover more about this movement in the following books: Neil Cole, *Organic Church: Growing Faith Where Life Happens* (Jossey-Bass, 2005); Neil Cole, *Church 3.0: Upgrades for the Future of the Church* (Jossey-Bass, 2010).

3   Alan Hirsch, *The Forgotten Ways*, (Brazos Press, 2006), p. 19.

4   "Christianity in China: How many Christians are in China?" http://www.billionbibles.com/china/how-many-christians-in-china.html .

CHAPTER 7: BEING DIFFERENT IN THIS DIFFERENT WORLD

1   Keith Giles, *Jesus Untangled: Crucifying Our Politics to Pledge Allegiance to the Lamb* (Quoir, 2017), p. 89.

2   Francis A. Schaeffer, *How Should We Then Live?* (Crossway Books, 2005).

3   As told to Thomas Friedman and recounted in *Thank You for Being Late*, p. 35.

4   Friedman, *Thank You for Being Late*, p. 35.

5   Ibid, p.33.

6   Douglas Belkin, "More Companies Teach Workers What Colleges Don't," *The Wall Street Journal*, March 22, 2018. https://www.wsj.com/articles/more-companies-teach-workers-what-colleges-dont-1521727200 .

7   As told to Thomas L. Friedman in an interview recounted in Friedman, *Thank You for Being Late*, p. 103.

8   Emily Dickenson, *Forever is Composed of Nows*, https://www.poetryfoundation.org/poems/52202/forever-is-composed-of-nows-690 .

9   Joshua Cooper Ramo, *The Age of the Unthinkable: Why the New World Disorder Constantly Surprises Us and What We Can Do About It* (Back Bay Books, 2010).

CHAPTER 8: SOME GOOD NEWS

1   Colossians 1:27.

2   Thomas L. Friedman, *The World Is Flat: A Brief History of the Twenty-First Century* (Farrar, Straus and Giroux; Expanded and Updated edition, 2006).

3   Jessica Leber, "You Are Connected To Everyone On Earth By Just 4 Degrees Now," Fast Company. http://www.fastcoexist.com/3020687/you-are-connected-to-everyone-on-earth-by-just-4-degrees-now .

CHAPTER 9: RIDING THE EXPONENTIAL WAVES

1   Walter A. Henrichsen, *Disciples Are Made-Not Born: Making Disciples Out of Christians* (Victor, 1985), p.143.

2   Steven R. Covey, *The 7 Habits of Highly Effective People: Powerful Lessons in Personal Change*, (Simon & Schuster 1989), p. 22.

3   That isn't to say that a specific gift doesn't produce more multiplication than others. The apostolic gift is given to the Church to lay a foundation of multiplication. Void of this gift, the Church can only grow via addition. Why? Because the apostolic gift distributes the power to be able to reproduce disciples to everyone. An *apostolos* (Greek for apostle) is a sent one and is the foundation for launching church movements. The sent one reproduces him/herself and sends.

4   Malcom Gladwell, *The Tipping Point: How Little Things Can Make a Big Difference* (Back Bay Books, 2002); Chip and Dan Heath's book *Made to Stick* is influenced by Gladwell's sticky terminology. Larry Osborne's *Sticky Church, Sticky Leaders* and *Sticky Teams* all use Gladwell's terminology.

5   Seth Godin, *Tribes: We Need You to Lead Us* (Penguin, 2008), p. 79.

6   Lewis Galantiere's full translation of the first two paragraphs of the third chapter (The Tool) of *Wind, Sand and Stars.*

CHAPTER 10: FINDING BETTER WAYS

1   Johannes P. Louw, Eugene A. Nida, *Greek-English Lexicon of the New Testament Based on Semantic Domains,* (United Bible Societies, 1988), p. 465.

2   In my book *Church 3.0: Upgrades for the Future of the Church*, I argue that both centralized and decentralized networks of churches can be healthy. I point out that there are advantages and disadvantages on either side of the spectrum…and that is true. We have good networks across the spectrum from very centralized to very decentralized in our organic church movement. That said, this book is about a pressing urgency: our lack of multiplication in a world where hostility to the things of Christ are likely to increase. We are very accustomed to a centralized model of church, and it is time for us to move along the spectrum, closer to decentralized. On the plus side of being decentralized is rapid multiplication and also resistance to persecution. It seems to me that our times demand that we start to make a move in that direction.

3   It is clear that while The Gospel of John follows Jesus' life, it is not ordered in a strict chronological order. It is put together more topically than the synoptic gospels. The miracles that John writes about are placed in an intentional order. Therefore, following the order as John intended, while not absolutely necessary, has advantages.

4   LTG app. https://itunes.apple.com/us/app/ltg/id947795532?mt=8 .

5   You can learn more about Life Transformation Groups with either of the following books (you will only need one): Neil Cole, *Cultivating a Life for God: Multiplying Disciples through Life Transformation Groups*, Reprinted 2014 (CMAResources). Or Neil Cole, *Ordinary Hero: Becoming A Disciple Who Makes A Difference*, (Baker Books, 2008). LTG Cards are available at our website: www. CMAResources.org, and for a limited time the book *Cultivating a Life For God* is available there as a free ebook. https://www.cmaresources.org/cultivating-a-life-for-god-ebook .

6   https://www.cmaresources.org/cultivating-a-life-for-god-ebook .

7   We highly recommend that the learners also have books from non-evangelical traditions, but these are in addition to the two main books they utilize.

8   Neil Cole, *TruthQuest Facititators Guide*, CMAResources.org https://www.cmaresources.org/truthquest-facilitators-guide .

9   Proverbs 27:17 NIV.

CONCLUSION: THE END OF THE BEGINNING

1   According to Peter Diamandis and Steven Kotler in their excellent (and overly optimistic) book *Abundance: The Future is Better Than You Think*, there are some sixty scientific analyses of the planet's capacity for population. Diamandis and Kotler, *Abundance*.

ABOUT THE AUTHOR

Neil Cole was born and raised in Los Angeles, California. While studying art as a freshman at California State University, Long Beach, he encountered the good news of Jesus Christ and turned his life over to Him, never looking back.

Neil's journey in God's Kingdom brought him to serve in a megachurch of over 3,500 people, a local community church of 120, and now as a catalyst to help start thousands of small, rapidly multiplying, organic churches that meet in homes, campuses, prisons, dormitories, and places of business across the globe. Neil has authored fourteen books and traveled to over forty-eight nations of the world, sowing the seeds of God's Kingdom, catalyzing the development of organic church networks, and coaching thousands of leaders and churches.

Neil has been married for thirty-five years to Dana and has three adult children—Heather, Erin, and Zach—and three grandsons.

Neil Cole regularly contributes to the following websites:

www.StarlingInitiatives.com
www.neilcole.blog
www.CMAResources.org
www.100movements.org
www.cole-slaw.blogspot.com

OTHER BOOKS IN THIS SERIES

Starling Initiatives Publications creates resources aimed at releasing followers of Christ to hear and respond to the voice of their Lord with immediacy, courage and without need of a human filter or a middle-man. Our motto is simple and significant: *Listen to Jesus and do what He says.* We believe that if all of us just did that, the world would change almost immediately. We continue to create resources to that end. Here are some:

The next book in the Starling Initiatives Publications Series (SIPS), *Sent*, addresses the apostolic gift. The apostolic gifting is the foundation we need in order to see rapidly multiplying movements of the gospel. It is the gift of empowerment that spreads the good news and catalyses movements. There is much confusion over the gift of the apostle, and the next book will bring much-needed clarity and a biblical perspective. This book will be available in the Spring of 2019.

Cultivating a Life for God: Multiplying Disciples Through Life Transformation Groups describes the simple and highly transferable concept of Life Transformation Groups. It is full of stories and examples as well as a thorough section addressing common questions. We offer this book in both print and electronic format.

TruthQuest: The Search for Spiritual Understanding is a community-based theological discovery system designed to equip leaders to continue the journey of lifelong learning. You can get both the Facilitator's Guide and Participants Workbook at our website.

www.CMAResources.org